About the Author

Graham Andrews is a professional writer and editor. He lives on the South Coast of New South Wales, where he has conducted online writing courses and tutored in writing. He has worked as consulting scientific editor, and as senior editor. This is Graham's ninth book.

Other Books By the Author

A Guide To Wrought Iron and Welding

You're On Air

In Your New Image

Easy Guide To Creative Writing

Easy Guide To Writing Winning Essays

Easy Guide To Science and Technical Writing

Island Of the Barking Dog

Dad Kept Bees

Reach For the Sky

Become the writer you have always wanted to be

Graham J Andrews

Flairnet

ISBN : 978-0-9924642-6-4

Published by Flairnet
www.flairnet.com.au

National Library of Australia Cataloguing-in-Publication entry

Creator: Andrews, Graham J., author.

Title: Reach for the sky : become the writer you have always wanted to be / Graham J Andrews.

ISBN: 9780992464264 (paperback)

Notes: Includes bibliographical references and index.

Subjects: Creative writing--Handbooks, manuals, etc.
Authorship--Handbooks, manuals, etc.
Radio authorship.
Fiction--Authorship.
Short story.

Dewey Number: 808.02

Contact the Author:
Email: graham@grahamandrews.com
Website: www.grahamandrews.com

Contents

Preface

I grew up in a house full of books.

My mother read the odd novel, my father was not interested in reading at all, and my brother ran the other way when he heard even a mention of books.

My father was a bookbinder, with a home-based job of repairing books for the suburban libraries in the city where I grew up.

Each month, when the cartons of books arrived at our house, I would be unpacking the first carton to see what was in it for me even before the last carton was brought inside.

The books were a real mixture — reference books that had been worn to bits through constant use, novels that had been enjoyed by many readers, and of course children's books. These were the delights in my life, from about age eight to about fourteen years old.

After going through every carton, and looking at every book, I would choose about twenty of those I liked best, and immediately set about reading them. I had only one month to read all those that interested me, so I didn't have time to waste. As I read each book, I realised that I wanted to write books too.

The time came when I had to decide what I wanted to do. I applied for positions as a journalist with a city newspaper, and was told that I was too old at eighteen. Yes, too old at that young age.

It was many years later before I had the opportunity to develop my writing skills and become the writer I had always dreamed of, enjoying the life that I had always dreamed of — enjoying my environment, doing something meaningful and creative.

Opportunities came to me early, but slowly, with one publishing contract by a leading publisher even before I had finished my formal studies, and requests to write for several magazines about the topic of my book.

Over time, I moved on, and developed an interest in radio, and in making things, and in writing — all of which were to become the topics of my articles and my books.

Several successful on-line writing courses helped people develop their skills in this area.

Sharing gives me pleasure, like the things I like with those around me who are also interested in those same things.

It is satisfying to help people achieve what they set out to do in their lives, as it is to work with people and encourage them. It is a pleasure when they write to me or send me an email and tell me they have had their latest story published, or have been accepted by a publisher.

Over the years, opportunities have disappeared for writers, while many new opportunities have developed, opportunities where anyone who has talent can write and be published.

The technology that has made this new scope possible is still evolving, giving writers even more opportunities to write, and see their books in print, and to develop anything associated with writing. The same new technology gives writers the chance to market their work, and to promote not only their writing, but themselves as writers.

This book, therefore, gives those people who are keen to learn to write and see their work in print, one more opportunity.

Introduction

Writing is many things to many people — it is an expression of their thoughts, it is developing those special skills they posses as storytellers.

Writing is a chance for a person to be heard, to have someone listen to what they have to say, to discuss with them their thoughts, their ideas about a topic of interest.

Whatever the motives of writers, most, if not all, write because it's that one thing that is so important to them at the time. That's all they want to do. That's all they want to be — a writer.

The one thing about readers is that they adore their books — they often prefer books to human company. Animal company seems to be different. Many readers sit in front of a fire reading, with a cat on their laps. Perhaps the two go well together.

People read for different reasons — they relate to the characters they are so engrossed in, and almost live the life of the person they are reading about. They like to get lost in another's world, a world of make-believe, or even a world of reality, seen through different eyes, and different experiences.

People read for entertainment, for amusement. Others read to inform themselves, to get a number of different points of view. If you have the same viewpoints as everyone else, then where do you go to discuss anything? Everyone has the same opinions about everything, and that certainly wouldn't make for an interesting world, would it?

People read to travel the world. A book costs a few dollars, world travel costs thousands of dollars. But in their books, and through their reading, they could be anywhere, as long as their imagination goes along with them in their reading.

Just as readers have so many different reasons for wanting to read, writers have so many different reasons for wanting to write.

No two writers will have exactly the same reason for what they do, although most would give one of perhaps no more than half a dozen reasons why they write. They might claim to write to earn money, but even with this as a reason, there are varying degrees of weighing up the work involved with the remuneration they could reasonably expect from their endeavours.

Other writers like to tell a story. They believe that their readers will get just as much delight out of reading the story as they themselves did in the telling the tale.

Some writers write because they have vivid imaginations. Others might even tell us that they would otherwise be unemployable. They probably would be! Can you imagine someone with a great gift of a storyteller, combined with great and unique ideas, sitting in a boring office, pushing a pen around a desk? Life doesn't work like that for successful writers. Perhaps they are right—they would otherwise be unemployable. Can you imagine a talented writer sitting there, gazing out through the window, waiting for the next boring meeting to start— perhaps one where their boss has called them in to discuss another meeting? Can you imagine a meeting to discuss a meeting? Wouldn't those writers rather be writing, using their skills and talents to the fullest? I am sure they would.

How many reasons do readers need to read a good book, and enjoy the creation of a storyteller? Do they even need an excuse?

How many reasons does a writer have to give to justify writing? Just because someone else cannot see merit in what they propose writing, this is no excuse for that writer to listen to them and not write. Writing is individual, and it is unique. It is unique to each and every writer. No two writers will write exactly alike, even though there are millions of good writers in the world. Each one has a story to tell, and if those millions of writers put their thoughts into their writing, they will come up with something that is truly themselves—millions of good ideas.

The world is full of great books. We have some beautiful and enduring literature. Some of the most popular books have been around for over two hundred years, and they are still in print. Others are very recent additions to the shelves of the world's bookshops and home libraries. All those great books started with an idea, and with a love of telling a story. They started with a passion—the passion of the writer to tell that story. To such writers, everything else in the world can wait. Writing comes first.

And have you noticed one thing about the results of those writers who have that attitude? The efforts result in literature that stands out. Their books are way ahead of those who write because ... well, I thought I would try something ... might give it a try ... see how I go ...

Those who are writers, write. They produce works that are not only worth writing, but they write books that are truly worth reading.

Libraries around the world hold huge numbers of books. All are original works. Yes, every single one of them! All are works of individuals. Every single one of them. All those books started with that same magic ingredient that makes a writer what he or she becomes.

They all started with an idea. They had that magic ingredient of enthusiasm. They had that ingredient of 'I must write this before I do another thing' attitude. The results are there for the whole world to see, and to read, and to appreciate.

When any writer is starting out in their new field of endeavour, there is one essential ingredient that will make a tremendous different to their success or failure. Unless they are very wealthy, or come from a wealthy family who believes in them and is prepared to support them for perhaps a rather long time, then they will need the full support of family. They have to eat, and their immediate family has to eat.

Even if you are successful early in your chosen endeavours, and get something accepted for publication, it can be a long time before you see that first cheque in the mail, or the amount the editor has conceded to give you, in your bank balance. You have, let's say, just written an article for a magazine. The editor has agreed to publish it. Your hopes are raised as high as it's possible to lift them. But you have missed the deadline for the next issue, as that is being compiled right now. And you won't make the following issue either because that is all planned, and there's no room for your masterpiece. So that is nearly nine months before it gets into print. And then, hopefully, when that issue is distributed to newsagents, you receive a free copy (if the editor is generous, or you might have to ask for the copy to which you are entitled), you get a cheque with the copy of the magazine containing your article.

Don't get too excited. Often payment is made at the editor's discretion. In other words, he or she will pay you the minimum amount they can get away with paying you. So after nine months, you might receive a cheque for perhaps three hundred dollars. You are naturally excited, but that won't buy you many cups of coffee while you wait for the next article to be published and you receive payment for it. It is then that you will realise that coffee beans are more economical rather than cups of coffee each time you go out. Such is the life of a writer.

But ... would any writer decide not to write based on the meagre payment received for a lot of work? Never. Writers write because that's what they want to do. They like to tell a story, to communicate, to work with words, and play with ideas. There are so many reason why people want to write, but not many reasons why they choose not to do so.

How good a writer they become is up to that individual. If someone writes out of mere duty, the result will be a boring, uninspiring collection of words. If they write with passion, then their readers will read it with the same enthusiasm. Now, isn't that worth striving for as you become the writer you have always wanted to be? I am sure it is.

Chapter 1 Writing Is an Individual Creation

Writing is an individual process. It doesn't require a huge team of writers to write a short story, a novel, or even a how-to book.

You will get the team effort in corporate-style writing, where everyone has to feel important and have their say. The results of team writing, however, are invariably a disaster, and the whole process takes ten time longer than if one person were to be assigned the task and was allowed to get on with the job. Unless one person edits the report or corporate or government document carefully, there will be ten different styles in the report, with ten different viewpoints.

Unfortunately, many people believe that because they are in a certain position of responsibility in an office, then no one else could possibly write just like them. But read their style. Often it's just ... boring. They are right there — not many people would really want to write just like them.

Many years ago a government department in Australia did write and publish a corporate report written by a team of writers. Many years later, that same report was used in all teaching classes as a splendid example of how not to write.

But the writing you will be working on, your own, individual projects, will all be done by one writer—you.

And that's what makes individual writing so enjoyable. The result—the end of the story or article—is all your own work. Wow! You should be proud of what you have achieved.

I once told a writer that even though their writing wasn't something they could use to win great prizes because it wasn't the greatest piece of literature, I did congratulate her because she had created something that the other twenty-two million people in Australia had never done, and possibly couldn't do (if they had been able to do so, I am sure they would have done so before then). So my writing friend had created something that was her own, and something that was unique to herself. Be yourself, with your own ideas, with your own feelings. Just be you. You are the artist, otherwise you wouldn't be embarking on this adventure into the world of creativity, and expanding on your thought, and developing your imagination. We owe it to others to tell that special story. After all, it won't write itself. And if you don't write that story that's on your mind, how do you know that someone else won't write it and claim all the credit for an idea shared with you?

If you love reading, then you should love writing. But get into the habit of reading too. Without a lot of reading behind you, your writing can't move forward very far. If you are to become a writer, how could you not enjoy reading? Who needs an excuse to read a lot of books?

One thing you can do to develop your writing style is

to read a lot. Read novels, read short stories, read lots and lots of magazine articles. Read romances, detective stories.

And then work out what you liked, and what you didn't like about everything you read. Most times, we don't bother to analyse the style of the writer whose work we are reading. We read it without much thought going into anything other than its content.

You will learn a lot about other writers' styles if you look at the good parts of their writing. Was it the short sentences you enjoyed? Was it the colourful expressions they used? Was it their use of short sentences and short paragraphs that made the information easy to read and easy to grasp?

Analyse what you read with enjoyment and consider why you liked it.

Although you will learn a lot about writing style by considering works that you enjoy, you will probably gain a lot more about style if you critically analyse work you don't enjoy.

It's like a shopping experience, or getting service from a business. You probably won't say much if you enjoyed the product or the experience, but most people will complain bitterly if they get an experience that they don't appreciate.

Decide what it was that you didn't like. Look critically at every paragraph, every sentence, and every word. Work out what it was that clashed with you.

Now, within those two realms — what you enjoyed and what you didn't like — is your answer that you should work on, and possibly what will work for you.

Don't copy one style. Just use it to guide you in

developing your own style. There is a difference between copying someone else's style and developing your own, even though you are using the same basic ingredients of other writers. After all, with millions of writers, and only a small number of individual styles, there will be overlap. But within that style, you will learn to be you — the writer you have always wanted to be.

You don't want a regurgitation of someone else's work. And you don't want to emulate someone else's style, or content, because if someone else had written exactly what someone thought you should write, the way they thought you should write it, then why should you even bother with the task of writing? Why haven't they done so before this, anyway?

Aim for originality. Aim to be yourself. And this is going to make you stand out from all the other writers. It is going to make your writing stand out from the mountains of other material that is written and published every year.

It's not too difficult to develop your own style.

A while back I was working with a writing student whom I felt had the potential to become a writer. She was almost there but not quite. I encouraged her, and once told her that one day she would find that it 'just happened'.

About a year later I received an email from her with a couple of short stories attached. And they were good. In fact they were really good.

In her note to me, she reminded me that I had told her that one day it would just happen, and then one day she realised what that magic ingredient was to turn something from the state of ordinary, to the state of really, really good.

It was herself, being herself. It was, really, as simple as that.

My student had allowed her thoughts to come across in her writing, in her own expressions. It was as if she was telling me a story. It wasn't the story where the writer is distant from the reader. It was as if the writer was there in front of me, talking to me.

How do you develop your own, unique style?

You might have struggled for a long time trying to write articles for different magazines. And then, one day, it 'just happens'.

You might be writing when you are in a jovial mood. That will come across in your writing style. You might feel passionate about something. Your enthusiasm will come across in your writing. That will be your style.

If you are disinterested in your topic, how do you expect readers to be interested in your composition? They won't be. They will have the same enthusiasm that you had — very little. So why bother if that's the best you can do? You won't enjoy the process of writing, and your readers won't enjoy the result of your effort.

When you write fiction — short stories, the novel, romance, the great detective story — you will be creating something new, and hopefully something great. But in particular, you will be creating something of your own. So learn to tell it just as you want to tell it.

Whatever you write, and whatever you do, you will be criticised. As far as criticism with your writing is concerned, that criticism will apply to you when you develop your style in writing. Others won't be able to write the same way, so they will have something to say. It is a pity people adopt such an attitude, because they could be far more productive if they did the same as what you are doing—writing their own novel, or romance, or telling about their experiences.

With so many incidents happening in our lives, and in the lives of those people all around you, there are so many stories to tell. Everyone has a story about their life's experiences, something that happened to them, a calamity, a divorce, a collapse of their business. Each person, if they were to write about such incidents in their own life, would tell the story in a different way. Isn't this what makes life interesting? No two ways of telling it will be exactly the same. These same authors would start their stories from different points in time, and from different viewpoints. Some would blame others for what happened to them. Others would see humour in their situation no matter how grim that event might seem to us. With so much happening in the world, and in individual lives, there is always room for an individual point of view.

People will leave out what others would consider important ingredients in their life's story. Others give the most minute details of everything. They will tell of the good things even in a sad situation and make the reader feel positive. If a writer can feel positive with so much going against them in life, that makes us feel good, doesn't it? Perhaps that is why we prefer some writers and some styles over those of others we have read.

Other people dwell on the unfortunate side of their circumstances, and the gloom and doom of all that is going on around them. Many readers enjoy that. There is a saying that good news never sells newspapers. So if your style were to include the less than bright side of life, then that's your own, individual style.

But no matter which side of the story you adopt, remember that life is full of good things that happen to us, as well as things that we would prefer not to have happened.

With your own writing style, you can always make those less than enjoyable moments in life happen to someone else in your work of fiction. It is your story you are telling, the way you want it to be told, so go ahead.

Whether you are writing fiction or non-fiction, a drama or a comedy, your personality should come across. Your voice is important in the writing process, so never be a mute. Say things as you want to say them, and the result you create will be far ahead of those boring public-service style reports that inspire no one.

One word of warning is called for here. In the Romantic Era of European writing, authors included a lot of detail in their narratives, and in all their descriptions. This created vivid scenes, and great settings. Every word of their literature said something, just as the author had intended.

If, however you use a lot of words to describe something, that is not to imply that those words are constructive in describing a setting or a scene. Lots of words in a novel that convey lots of meaning and lots of information are fine. Blatant ramblings are not acceptable. If you need to say in ten sentences what could easily have been said in one short sentence, then you are failing as a writer, and you are failing your readers. If you use a lot of prose, make sure the content is valid, and is necessary.

Necessity is the key to successful writing. If the words are justified, then use them. If those extra words (or sentences) don't add one single bit of extra information or detail, then don't use them.

Through good editing of your work, you will be able to cut out all those that are unnecessary.

The key to good writing is, to a large extent, deciding on which words to keep, and those you can throw out without losing anything from the message. Good writing comes down to good editing.

It is often in the editing of your work that your true voice will come across and be honed so that readers can really say, 'yes, that is definitely you — I recognise you now'.

Chapter 2 What's It All About?

Congratulations. You have made that first step to what many people regard as a great way of life, creating a lifestyle many only dream of. But for many, that ideal lifestyle will remain only a dream.

Or perhaps you have already dabbled in a bit of writing, have earned a taste for it, and want to take the craft further. Again, congratulations.

Throughout this book, I am going to give you many ideas about writing, about how you can achieve success in writing, and show you just what is attainable by being a writer.

But I will also show you that writing is not necessarily the most lucrative occupation there is. Many, many writers would find it more financially rewarding to be on unemployment benefits than to try to earn a good income from writing. But this should not deter those who want to be a writer, no matter how much, or more likely, how little they could expect to earn from their writing.

Why write? Why would people want to become a writer? At a dinner one evening, one of the guests asked me why I write. Do you enjoy it? There's always someone who will ask silly questions. Another asked if I could write about enough things without sounding boring. Could I write about something I had little interest in? That really started the evening's discussion. Silly people!

I write because I love working with words. They are my expression to the world. I'm no good with convincing arguments with the spoken word. I can't think of the right arguments at the right time. Those choice things come to me too late, when the impact of those spoken gems has truly passed. I write because words are my voice to the world. I can express myself in print, or on the World Wide Web. I write words that are easily understood, by those I enjoy writing for.

I write because I like working with colour — the colour of words, the colour of the scenes I create, the colour of the photographs I take to illustrate my articles, or the websites I develop.

I write because I can combine all this with other activities that I really enjoy, like cycling, photography, and making things.

I ride a bike — a hundred kilometres or so on a Sunday, and sometimes during the week, because that's what I enjoy doing. I write about cycling and the bike rides, of riding to a headland to watch the whales. I ride to a beach where I have the beach to myself for a couple of hours, and let my mind be receptive to any thought that dare enter it, to be churned around and turned into an article or, better still, a story.

I like to write about cycling because I enjoy sharing, sharing enjoyable times, those special moments with others who also have a passion for what they enjoy.

Because I am out there, thoroughly enjoying myself, the words come with such enthusiasm, and with the right amount of colour, and the right amount of expression to make them interesting and meaningful.

Another author might write because she wants to reveal the experiences and encounters in her life, to make sense of her own thoughts and perceptions, to interpret how they influence her. It brings together all aspects of life — the confusion, the sameness, the excitement, the challenges, the sadness. Other authors write because they can live through the life of their characters.

Creative writing is about the motivations of a character in our stories, about the impressions they leave on us, and the places our characters travel. While we read, often we take on the thought of our favourite characters in the book. It's the same when we write about a character. For the moment, we are living through that person, real or imaginary.

Somewhere, somehow, writers hope to reach out to others through their writing to share in those experiences and thoughts and find the connections we all share with one another.

Some writers have taken up writing in desperation, when everything else they did had failed, and they were at rock bottom in their lives. Surprisingly, some became famous authors. Others have struck gold in their writing when they thought they didn't have anything else to offer.

Others write to record their thoughts, like in a journal as they pass from one day to the next in their travels that is called life. Perhaps they write to motivate themselves.

Writing gives meaning and purpose to the sometimes complex and intertwined and convoluted experiences.

Other writers find comfort, or great solace in the words that they write.

Writing has turned them into the person they now are. They eventually identify themselves with their writing ... they are writers ... creators of something fresh and original.

Writing helps us understand what we are made of, giving a form to thoughts that seem otherwise difficult to understand. Emotions, thoughts, guilt, feelings that run through our lives and experiences in our own worlds can often be overwhelming. Finding words to express our thoughts can help us make sense of them, and can help us to learn who we really are.

Just as no two lives are ever completely alike, and no two characters, or those that writers create, are ever alike, no two reasons why writers want to write will ever be the same. We are individuals, with our own ideas, our own thoughts, our own way of doing things. But ... somewhere between, perhaps, all our paths cross eventually ... those real life paths, and those of our characters that are in some way ourselves coming out into the real world. We experience things differently, and see things differently from other writers.

All writers have one thing in common. We all like to share life with others that we call our readers. We like to let them into our own little worlds.

Now you know why some are driven to put pen to paper or to put their fingers on their computer's keypad. What about you?

What is writing to you?

Writing is more than just a means to earn money. If you can do that too, you are lucky. But writing is many things to different people.

Writing can be fun, and it can be enjoyable. It can be frustrating too. In the end, if you have achieved a certain degree of success, you should feel very proud of yourself, because you are far ahead of those who only wish to be a writer, but do nothing about developing their skills. If you develop that latent talent, then you can expect many rewards that are, together, far greater than the monetary value to be derived from this skill.

Writing is communicating. We communicate ideas, instructions, or with the right type of writing make someone's life more fulfilling, giving inspiration and motivation with sound advice. Perhaps the advice might be based on a lot of good ideas you have learned from a lifetime of meaningful living.

Other writing might be intended to educate, or to instruct.

What about humour? We all need a good laugh in our lives. Humour lifts our spirits, makes us feel happy. When we are happy, then we can achieve so much more, because our whole spirit goes into our everyday activities. Humour is not for everyone. Fill a room with people, tell some jokes, and you will find that a lot of people will laugh at a good joke, but you will get some who don't see it, don't want to see the funny side to life, and couldn't care less about having their spirits lifted for even a few minutes. Ah well, you win some ...

There are so many other types of writing. Magazines are full of articles for different readers. Can you relate to the contents of a particular magazine, and perhaps write articles that are every bit as good as those you have enjoyed? Probably you could.

There's even more about writing in the following pages. Much more about using words. There's also writing for the new media, including websites. If businesses don't have a website to promote their activities, then they effectively don't exist in the twenty-first Century. It's as simple as that. Aren't some of the websites terrible? The information conveyed to the reader is appalling, it's full of grammatical errors, spelling errors, and much of it just doesn't make sense. But that's something we will be looking at together later in this book. Good websites need good writers to write text. And nowadays, a static website loses its ranking on the main search engines very quickly. They soon drop down from the first page or two of the search engine results and disappear into oblivion. Blogs can keep websites fresh, and adding new content on a regular basis can be used effectively in maintaining the position of that website in the search engine results. Blog writing is a very effective means of earning quite a good income from writing. Many people can't write good blogs. Others see it as cost-effective to get someone else to write blogs for them. More of that too later on.

In the current age of technology, many people seem to think that the written word is becoming less popular and almost redundant. This is not so. There are still technical reports to be written. Corporations can't find good writers who can put together their material (sometimes it's nothing but corporate propaganda, but that's a different genre), and reports are not written in the best way they could be.

If the companies pay to get the text professionally written, they pay a lot of money for good service. That's where writers are needed. A good writer can achieve success in this field. It's just the presentation of the data that has changed over recent years. Instead of a company report being mailed out to all the shareholders, many companies save money and have it available online. This not only saves the company a fortune in printing costs, but also on postage. The cost of printing half a million copies of a coloured report is exorbitant. To add to that the cost of posting it out, well, you would be looking at another few million dollars each year to get the message out there.

Magazines over recent years have changed. Thirty years ago I was earning a good income from writing for a range of magazines. That's all changed. Although the magazines are still produced (a few of them no longer exist), they still contain articles. Many magazines, on realising that their revenue has been reduced because it is so difficult to attract appropriate advertisers, are trying to cut costs. Magazine articles are now staff written. That means one of the magazine company's own staff writing most of the material. But those staff members still needed training in writing, and experience in writing.

Another drawback with writing for magazines these days is that often the payment is at the editor's discretion, which means that if the editor likes the article you submit very much, he will use his discretion as to whether he pays you or not. If you write an article for a magazine and it is published without any form of payment other than a free copy of the magazine, then regard that as experience, put the printed copy in your portfolio of published work and move on.

Working as a journalist for a newspaper provides opportunities to develop valuable writing skills. With the demise of many newspapers these days, this might be an area that will prove difficult to break into in the future. There are a lot of journalists who are not gainfully employed. They might not even be employed. Revenue from advertising has dried up, their income has been decimated, and many newspapers are only just struggling to survive, especially with the new digital media taking over from the world that printed magazines and newspapers enjoyed for so many years.

I can see the point of advertisers. Why pay thousands of dollars on advertising in a newspaper or in a magazine, get limited returns, when they can get better results from the Internet, through social media, their corporate websites, and other means of effectively selling their goods online? It makes sense to pull out of the print media and radio and television advertising and concentrate on the new media that is giving good returns for a fraction of their previous costs.

So far, you should have got a taste of some of the more popular areas where writers are needed. Let's look at the craft of writing.

With writing, you can be, indeed should be, yourself. If you are a creative person, then writing is a splendid opportunity to show your talents to the rest of the world.

To the rest of the world, I can hear you say. Yes, to the rest of the world. These days, with the Internet, effective websites, e-mails, blogs, there is no such thing as a small, local community. At least there shouldn't be.

I have a number of published articles on my personal website. By using the user statistics, it is possible to trace where the people are coming from to read the material I have written. The small global village is now enormous. For my articles on growing trees for firewood, and burning wood effectively for maximum energy, I have hundreds of readers every month from the United Kingdom, from the United States, and many other countries. For a series of welding articles, I get site visitors from the US military, from the US general population, from all over Europe, as well as from my home country of Australia.

To write for a small magazine with a limited distribution is one thing. To write something for the Internet, you are reaching out to a potential of many millions of readers if the content of your writing is exactly what they want to read.

This use of site statistics points out that people are looking for information, for factual material. How great is that demand for your potential writing? It's enormous.

For material published on the Internet, there is huge potential for getting an enormous readership. Readership is what every writer is seeking. There is no point in writing a single word unless lots of people want to read everything you have written. So how does that inspire you to become a writer?

When I look back over the years and consider the frustration of finding magazines who wanted to pay me for articles that would make them money from selling advertising to go with my articles, to what can be achieved with far less frustration, one certainly would not want to return to the past. With writing, the past is gone. It's dead.

It's there to show us how it used to be done in the past. But we no longer live in the past. We live in the present, and that's where it is exciting, full of fresh ideas, where fresh markets present themselves on an almost daily basis. Wow! Bring on the future!

Writing magazine articles is not the only field of writing that has changed for the better in the twenty-first Century.

With the first book I had published nearly thirty years ago, I had to send a letter to a lot of publishers to see if they would even be interested in what I wanted to write. If they were, then I would send off a submission including everything about the book I wanted to write, how I saw their efforts to market it, and so on.

My second book earned an advance on my royalties of two hundred and fifty dollars. It took two and a half years for the publisher to finally get around to publishing the book even after I had signed the contract.

I still had to market the book they published. Without the Internet, I was limited as to what I could do.

Then the time arrived when publishers would only work through literary agents. They were the people who would sift out the manuscripts before the publisher even saw them.

That's changed too. Publishers are limited in number, and many have been amalgamated with even bigger publishers. And in the latest move, huge publishers have closed their doors and are no longer in the business. Penguin has just merged with Random House. And so goes the demise of traditional book publishing.

And in comes the new publishers—you! Yes, that's right. You can be your own publisher of great books, and marketed according to your best methods. Now there's no longer the need to write endless submissions and send off query letters, wait months for a rejection of your good idea, and then to start the placement business all over again, or to go through literary agents. You write a book, but make sure it is a good book, get it professionally edited because people don't want to read a collection of mistakes, and publish it yourself. You are not only a writer, but you are now a book publisher too.

This book will show you how easy it is (despite many authors telling you that it is far from easy) to write and publish and market your own book. In less time and for possibly far more royalties than you would have got from traditional publishers.

If you want to produce a newsletter about your favourite field of interest, don't get one printed each month and post it out, although the post office won't appreciate my telling you that any more than the local printer will appreciate my suggestion. Web-based newsletters are the way to go for many writers old and young.

Because of the potential reach of websites, many businesses and large companies will see more merit in advertising on your website, or on your newsletter, or on your web-based series of articles, than they do in paying a lot of money for limited readership, limited effectiveness (print advertising attracts only about two percent of the readership, of which an even smaller portion of readers responds to any particular advertisement).

If you write a radio script that is as involved as the most gripping movie, there is nothing to stop your publishing it on the web and getting people who might be interested in it (after you have given them the first few pages for free) to download the full script for a few dollars. From that point, they are free to produce your script on their own local community radio station.

You can have subscription-based magazines too, full of colour, and some advertising to pay you for your time. An on-line magazine can be as varied and as interesting as you can make it. As it is your own work, and all your own creation, there is no-one telling you what you should include in it, or to leave out. You are the creative person, you take charge of your production. And you set the price you ask readers to pay you for downloading it each month.

So whether you want to write a how-to book (still very popular), a novel, a series of articles about a particular theme, a book about radio dramas, or getting the best results from gardening in poor soil, the potential is there for your taking.

Don't you just kick yourself when you are out walking, or on the train going to work, and that brilliant gem of an idea comes to you and you know you must use it in your book? When you get to your destination and you go to write down that piece of literary brilliance, you find that it's gone. You can't remember it, or if you can, you can't capture the right feel of those words.

That's why you must carry around with you a small notebook. If the notebook is always with you, then you can jot down the passage that came to you earlier on, and capture the true feel of that piece. You might not use it immediately, but it might surprise you sometimes years later how useful that gem could become.

Write it down, and keep it. Keep it until you use it.

Hopefully you will be writing more than one piece, or article, or more than one play. That's when you will go through your notebook and find those gems.

Sometimes those few lines are so good they might even be the opening for an article or a newsletter you want to write. So it's worth writing them all down, and keeping them.

My record for keeping and using a gem is a little over twenty-five years. I couldn't see how I could use it until that one day when I needed just such a thought. On that occasion, it became the opening line of an article. The rest of the article flowed so smoothly that it was almost a matter of the opening that had been in my notebook for all those years finally wanting to be written and included.

How do you find interesting topics to write about?

A topic must be of interest to you. If it isn't, then it will be very difficult to write with much enthusiasm. That wouldn't be very good for your readers, would it?

Try this.

Create a list. It doesn't matter how long it is. Include all the things you love doing, and the things you enjoy in your everyday life. Let's say this list contains a range of activities. We can start with writing, because that is the reason why you are reading this book.

Other categories could include photography, and physical activities such as bush walking, canoeing, cycling, making things, cross-stitching, sewing and knitting. Okay, that's a start, but never rule off this list. Keep it open in case you think of anything else to add in coming months.

Now create a second list of all the things you are good at doing. They don't have to be work related, but just include all those things that you are good at doing. The items in this list are probably not going to be the same as those item in the first list. Unless of course, you enjoy doing everything you are good at doing.

Let's say this list of yours includes things like web design (creating an attractive website). To the list you might add activities or areas of your work, such as carpentry, or welding, and hopefully quite a few others.

Now put the two lists side by side.

Things I love to do	Things I am good at
Writing	Computer work
Photography	Website design
Bush walking	Welding
Canoeing	Carpentry
Snorkeling	Making pavlovas
Cycling	Making pickles
Playing the guitar	Making things

Now look at what happens if we combine two, three or more of these categories.

We could perhaps have writing combined with making things, combined with pavlovas. Do you want to be known as a specialist in making pavlovas? Here's your chance.

What happens if we combine writing and photography from the first list, and website design? A good website will have a combination of all three of these ingredients. It will be of a good design, combined with a good, clear text, and enhanced with the selection of a few good photographs.

Say we combine writing, photography, with bush walking. There's a possibility for a small book on interesting family bush walks in your area. A selection of twenty or so walks would result in a book that is suitable to be put into a backpack.

Now try combining writing, photography, cycling (three items on the list of things you love doing), with website design. There's a good chance for you to create a website on some of the great bike rides in your local area that others can enjoy on their outings. You are combining your love of writing, you are illustrating the website with interesting photographs to entice others to follow the path you have blazed for them, and, of course, cycling itself. Get sponsorship for this, get advertisers to list their accommodation or cafes that serve good coffee to cyclists on your site, and you have a steady stream of income for at least a few years.

Now wasn't that enjoyable, going out taking photographs along some of your favourite bush walks or bike rides, writing the text that accompanies the pictures, and putting it all together knowing that this is exactly the material others want to read? You are providing your readers with the type of information they want, and at the moment they want it.

What are the topics of interest and the topics on your 'good at' list? It is important never to rule off these two lists. Our interests do change over time, so what might not be an interest today could very well become the topic of an article, a book or a website in the near future.

If you start compiling that list now, then by the time you have come to the end of reading this book, you will have at least a selection of topics you will want to write about with enthusiasm.

A friend once gave me something he had written. I read the first couple of paragraphs and gave it back to him. 'Why are you giving me this to read?' I asked him.

He had forgotten the magic ingredient of good writing. He had forgotten to identify the most important person in the whole writing equation. He hadn't consider the reader. He just wrote ... well, something ... he wasn't sure what ... and neither was anyone else ... and he thought of himself as a writer.

Consider your reader. Identify your reader. Write for your reader, not for yourself, although hopefully you will get enjoyment from the process. What is your reader likely to be interested in? Why? At what level is his or her skill likely to be? Once you have identified your reader, then write for that person. Now we can move on.

Chapter 3 Where Can You Write?

A t least if you have got this far into this book, then obviously I haven't turned you right off wanting to become a writer.

So where can you work on these literary gems, and those pieces that you have decided you want to write?

The answer is ... anywhere you feel comfortable.

I have a little book written by Eric Maisel. It's titled *A Writer's Paris*. I have read it three times, and am about to read it for the fourth time.

Many people find Paris is a magical city, full of inspiration, characters, settings, plots, indeed everything is there that could possibly inspire a new or an experienced writer.

I can relate to that little book, because I have come away from Paris with the same feeling — that Paris really is a great place to write.

There are parks, big and small. There are gardens, with lots of people, thus lots of characters just waiting and wanting to be included in your next novel. There are little cafes where you can enjoy a coffee and a croissant while you write a thousand words.

And of course you have the Seine, that river with its colourful boats, that runs right through Paris. It has gardens and parks and benches and seats all along the main part that flows through Paris ... just waiting for you to go along with your tablet and start writing your next work. There are museums with their coffee shops. There are galleries also with their coffee shops. And usually plenty of seats for you to find just enough space to spread out and start writing.

Even if you are not the world's fastest typist, you should be able to manage one thousand words in first draft form while you have a coffee and a cake.

Just walking along that river gives many creative people the inspiration to want to go back to their apartment and start composing the words and turn them into something meaningful. Or better still, to sit beside the Seine and begin each day writing their book.

Paris really is a cultural centre. The people of France love their books. They love their writers. Recently the government wanted to raise the VAT on books. There was such a scream from the public — how dare you, they told the president. Books are our culture. Leave them alone! Even though the VAT on books is small compared with that on general goods, that didn't stop the people from screaming loudly about the imposition on their culture.

But not everyone is lucky enough to be able to go to Paris to write. Not everyone would want to go there. One word of warning though when in Paris, make sure your tablet, your phone and anything else that looks attractive is secured to you with a chain and padlock. Things can disappear from in front of you very quickly, very silently!

But the book does give the reader an insight into the many possible locations for writing, the ways writers can become even more creative.

There are so many other places that are suitable for your creativity.

Some people are inspired by the hustle and bustle of a busy office. That gets them going and enables them to be creative. If that sounds like you, that's great.

But look at other places too that are close to home.

Have you a quiet room in your house that would let you concentrate on writing and not be disturbed for an hour or so every day? If you do have the luxury of such a space, then use it, and make sure that others in your household really appreciate that that time really is yours and yours alone, when you are allowed get on with that one important thing in your life right now — writing your next work, whatever it might be.

But other people really have to understand that 'I need peace and quite for the next hour' really means 'I need peace and quiet for the next hour ... so please, everything else can wait, and I really will do all those chores you asked me to do last week, when I have written my thousand words for the day.' In other words, don't allow yourself to be disturbed. If you are, then move somewhere else where it is possible for you to concentrate on that important task you have set yourself. And please remember, writing, to you, is important, while others might not see the task in quite the same way.

Do you have a park nearby? Perhaps one that has tables

and benches where you can spread out and put your notes and your tablet or notebook in front of you and just think, and create? Being alone generally draws out the creativity in people. Listen to the birds, the ocean waves, or the wind in the trees, or whatever the prevailing sounds of the park might be.

When I go to a park to write, I take a thermos of tea or coffee and treat myself to the luxury of having a hot drink or two while I enjoy my creative moments. In the right setting, it is often difficult to decide which is the more inspiring moment — that of writing, or that of being alone.

Is that really the life of a writer, I can hear you asking?

Yes, for some writers — many writers — it really is their lifestyle.

Do you enjoy long walks through the forest? They can be inspiring too. Take a small portable recorder with you, and as you think up the next idea, record your thoughts into the device. Scale down the sides of hills, or listen to the birds in their native forest. They won't mind sharing their world with you as long as you are quiet and let them get on with performing their courtship displays. I live right next to a forest, where I take long walks. I am lucky enough to hear lyrebirds performing their full repertoire of mimicking all the forest sounds, including the calls of many other forest birds. I often think the lyrebirds sound better than the real birds they are imitating.

The small, portable sound recording devices these day are very handy if you use them in situations like this. They will often capture the sounds of the forest, as well as your own voice. And with voice recognition software available now (often the software comes with the device when you buy it), you don't even need to retype your creative effort. Load it into your computer, plug in the recorder, and it will transcribe your voice into text on the page right in front of you! You will need to edit the text heavily, and make sure it puts down the words you actually spoke, not those it thinks you said.

I am lucky enough to live by the ocean too, one of my dreams that came true for me many years ago when I first started to be a writer. To me, there is nothing nicer than sitting on a headland overlooking the ocean with the waves breaking on the rocks below, drinking my hot cup of tea, and being that creative person I had always wanted to become. Can you imagine it ... a writer, looking at the ocean, no one else around, no houses, drinking a cup of tea or coffee, getting inspired to write, and putting down a couple of thousand words into my tablet.

I realise not everyone lives close to the ocean, nor would the ocean inspire them as much as it does with me. So let's look at some other possible writing venues for you.

Do you enjoy some sort of physical activity — cycling perhaps, or jogging?

I wrote a book on my way into work each day several years ago. I would cycle the forty-five minutes to the office (it was quicker to ride a bike than it was to catch the bus). During that ride into work, I would compose a thousand words in my mind. And because I was not distracted or slowed down by having to type the words at the time, I could think much faster and compose the words in my mind as I rode along past the lake.

I would get to work before anyone else did, and would type those words on my computer at work, and email them to my home computer.

And on my return journey, I would do the same. I knew exactly what I wanted to say, and how I wanted to say it. Before long, the sixty thousand words were completed. Painlessly. And while I enjoyed something as much as cycling around the lake.

But for you, you may develop some other creative way to write.

It is important not to just sit at home where you might not be inspired and try to force those words out of the computer. It won't work that way. It seldom does.

So what can you do that is truly different that is going to enable you to be creative? You will be looking for an activity or an environment that is quiet, perhaps not one you are accustomed to in your everyday life, and one that allows you to be yourself. After all, all good writing comes from those who are really being themselves, writing what they want to say, and in the style they want to write it.

A friend of mine rewards himself every day. If he feels he has earned it (and this is reward for achieving something that he considers worthwhile with his time), he goes down the road, sits in a coffee shop having a coffee and a cake or a salad roll. And he takes his tablet with him, and achieves his writing success in an environment where he is comfortable, and where the ideas are able to come to him at the same rate at which he can type them.

If we tell our minds just what we want them to come up with, and forget the idea, the mind seems to take heed and compose something worthwhile even when we are not even thinking about the task consciously. Now that's a great way to write!

Imagine telling your mind to write. Give it some idea of what you want it to come up with to guide it in the right direction and then let it do the work for you. That's how I write my most creative work. I set off from home on a long bike ride along the coast of about a hundred kilometres return trip. I tell my mind what I want to write as soon as I leave home, and let it do the rest. It might be the text for a website, or the text for a blog to promote something on a website. Or it might be promotional material I am writing for the local newspaper, or better still, the chapter of my next book.

And then I forget about it until the next morning.

When I take out the computer in the morning, all I have to do is type. I correct the numerous typos and make sure that the work is complete. Writing in this manner does take a little practice, but if this is your chosen location for writing, then it is worth the time to train your mind to do the work for you. You won't have to consciously struggle over every word you write.

Okay, I can hear you saying again that you don't cycle, and have nowhere nice to go. That's alright, so now we will consider some alternative spots for your creativity.

Remember, the more inspiring the location you choose for your writing, usually the more creative will be the result. After all, how can you hope to be creative if your surrounds don't allow it? It doesn't work that way.

Most towns, and just about all cities, have parks. They are not always a hundred kilometres from your work place. So go there at lunchtime, take your lunch, your hot drink, your tablet or notebook, and spend an hour in the park. There will be other people there too, but they will be getting on with their activities. If they didn't plan to enjoy themselves in the peace and the quiet of the local park, then they wouldn't have gone there. So if you can find somewhere to sit, perhaps at a table because it is convenient, or lean yourself against a large tree and sit in its shade, you should be able to write perhaps a thousand words.

Even if you allow time to enjoy your lunch, drink your hot drink, and look around you, you will still have time to write five hundred words. These are good words I am talking about, the right words. So, with five hundred words each day, five days a week, and a target of sixty thousand words (enough for around a two hundred-page book) you will take only twenty-four weeks to complete your manuscript. If you can mange one thousand words each lunch time, then cut this time down to only twelve weeks, or a little under three months.

Now, how long have you been making excuses for not starting that manuscript, under the excuses of no suitable place to write, no time and all the other etceteras that writers are good at creating? If you are like just about all other writers, then you could have written at least ten manuscripts, or books, in the time you had been thinking you had nowhere to write that first book, and no time to write it. Remember that a book, or whatever it is you are writing, perhaps a stage play or a radio drama, is never written in one sitting. It will take weeks, months sometimes, to write the required amount of words. So if you find somewhere to write, then go there and start writing.

So you still have nowhere that is conducive to writing

that masterpiece? Let's look at even more possibilities. I have exhausted the exciting venues for inspiring creativity, so what remains may not be exactly what I would choose for myself, but hopefully are worth considering anyway.

If you go to a place that is different—a park perhaps, or a small cafe—look around at all the ideas there. There might be wrought-iron brackets, or interesting lamp posts, or a door of a cafe that is of a rather creative design. Just remember that someone who was also creative came up with the ideas for those items, and their creativity was inspired by something else.

So why not look at something that might at first seem rather ordinary, and wonder about all the features of the place—the setting, the table, the park benches, the lamp posts, the arrangement of the gardens surrounding the coffee shop.

Inspiration instils inspiration in others. So if you see a creative feature, you are at least in an area where there were other creative people before you.

This is why it is not a good idea (usually) to remain back at work for an hour in the hope that you will have peace and quite to write. You will usually have the time, but your surrounds are seldom conducive to that level of creativity that you should aspire to.

A train journey at the end of the day after work might not at first appear to be the best place to write something creative. Really?

Public transport, combined with a mind that is allowed to run free, can be the perfect place for one type of writing—plot and character development.

Look at the person across the aisle from you on the

journey home today. Are they what they seem? Perhaps not, and this is where you can create all sorts of devious, mysterious people that you can put in your next work of fiction. Why is that man looking at his watch every minute or two? What is he anticipating? What's he up to? What has he planned? He looks that evil type, you realise (it's funny the things your mind can create!). So put that evil person in a setting. He's not going home, is he? So where is he going? Come on, get that imagination working for you – you have only another fifteen minutes before he gets off the train to carry out his dastardly deeds that you have planned for him.

Or that person in front of you in the supermarket queue. That person is not real, I can assure you. They might look like a genuine person, but only until you put mischievous ways into his make-up, and then you can manipulate him as much as you want to, make him do whatever your creativity wants him to do, make him carry out all your actions as if you were controlling a robot.

So don't let moments on public transport appear to you to be wasted. They need not be if you are creative, and are working on a creative work, such as a short story, or a series of short stories for your next book, or perhaps a longer work such as a novel or a detective story.

But we still haven't found you that perfect work environment for your creative spirits. So let us look at other options where you might be able to write.

Here's something you might be able to try.

Sit in front of a bookshop if you have one in your town or city. Lunchtime is a good time for this activity, because there are usually lots of people about. Sit on a bench in front of the bookshop and write. Just write, but imaging that it is your book those people are going into the bookshop to buy (and why wouldn't they?) After all, I am sure you could probably write a lot better than the authors of some (or is it many?) of the books that are published these days. Although mainstream publishers seem to be winding down their activities, many small bookshops are still around, and it looks like they will be there for many more years yet — certainly if they have new authors like yourself. But don't let this distract you from your creativity, because although those doors of the publishers are closing, many other doors are about to open for you ... just keep reading to find out more.

So imagine people going into that bookshop to buy your book. They could well be doing so in the very near future.   The thought of those people going in to the bookshop and browsing — perhaps for your own book next month or next year — is a real inspiration for any would-be authors to forget about the lack of suitable sites they have around them to instil creativity, and just start writing, and keep going until they have finished.

Don't forget one important fact. The authors of all those books in that bookshop probably didn't have any better place to write than the one you have singled out for yourself. They might not have been any different than you are. They might not have had any talents greater than those that you have. What each and every one of those other authors did possess, though, was the clear vision to see their book printed, and stocked in book stores, and people buying them, and reading them and enjoying them.

So, if all other locations fail, sit in front of the bookshop.

If that doesn't work, then please keep reading. Hopefully, the rest of the book will inspire you to write creatively.

Chapter 4 Creative Writing

There are seven billion people on earth right now, and each one of us has a story to tell. For some of us it might be a personal account of some tragedy, for others it is a fictional account of an incident in their lives, written as a story but based on some part of their experience.

Some writers who have a good imagination and are creative can take any little incident and turn it into a work of art. They can tell a story through creative writing that grabs the readers' attention as they turn the pages to see what happens next.

For the rest of us, and that includes the majority of us, we write because we want to. We want to show off our creativity, and we want to become storytellers. And so we shall.

Writing is something that can be learned, and it is something that can be taught. Creative writing is one aspect of writing that is both learned and is taught, combined with the storyteller's imagination, their personal skills to turn a story into that special piece of literature that the world wants to read.

So what is fiction, or creative writing?

Creative writing is often about the human experience, told from one point of view, to entertain the readers. It's often a personal story, maybe one that's based on fact but fictionalised to beef up life's otherwise mundane activities and results.

Creative writing could be based on cultural values, and cultural differences and cultural conflicts.

If a person is passionate about writing, I encourage them to put the ideas down and share their experience with their readers if the result is good enough. After all, it's your story you are telling, and you are the best person in the world to tell it. How could anyone else have exactly the same ideas, the same emotions as you do about an aspect of life? The direction each action takes in life for each of us will be different. The results of something that we call an everyday experience will be a turning point for some, routine for others. It's in the way that you tell your story that the real difference will be noticed.

Because all fiction is the work of individual minds, or in other words, the creation of an individual mind, it should be unique.

With those seven billion people, all with their stories to tell, there is going to be a tremendous overlap in stories. There are only a certain number (actually very few) original love stories. There are very few crimes that have not yet been committed. There are only a certain number of ways one can murder someone, or live a life of chaos. But it is in the telling of that story that is going to be important, and that is going to turn you into a good storyteller.

For creative writing, you need only a few ingredients. You will need characters. Without characters, you will have no story to tell.

You will need a plot — that's where everything happens. Without an interesting plot, nothing happens, and you won't have a story to tell.

And you will need a setting. Without a setting, you won't have anywhere for the characters to mess up, and you won't have anywhere to set your plot. So without a setting, or location, your story will also fail.

The three ingredients are brought together. It's the way you bring these three components together that will make a difference to your readers' experiences.

Everyone in life has much to say about everything. They all have opinions about everything — even, dare I say, about things that don't even concern them. In creative writing, your characters will say something from time to time. Others will say plenty all the time. And there will be those you create who use the minimum number of words to get their own message across and say very little, but they will still be effective in your story. In real life, we often get a mixture of such people. In your story, you can create a mixture of such people too to make the story realistic.

CONFLICT

When you bring two or more people together, you will eventually have conflict. This could be caused by different opinions, opinions on the way things should be done, or whole circumstances that should have been handled differently. In any work of fiction, your characters will need to do something. Make them the perfect lovers. Make them stir up everyone who comes their way. Make them angry with everyone. They might be always fighting amongst themselves. Do your characters have goals? That might be a source of conflict with the rest of the characters, especially if those have not changed in their lives since the day they left school sixty years earlier. Make all your characters do what you set out for them to do.

If you have finished your first draft and realise that you have included one or two strays in your work — those who have done very little, those who have not contributed in any significant way to the story, then run the delete button over them. If they don't serve a worthwhile role in your story, then you can be sure they have no place being there. So be prepared to delete, delete, and then delete. If, however, you like those characters in your story, keep them, keep their dialogue, and their personalities, and see if you can use them in a subsequent story. They might fit in better there, and have a more important role to play in story number two, or story number three.

With those ingredients of your story, it is important to remember that it is the originality of your story that is going to be important. Make your characters be entirely themselves. Make them behave in their own way. To give your readers something unique, you must be original. Be creative. Tell your story your way, the way you want it to be told. Although you probably won't come up with a new theme or a new plot, there is nothing to stop you, if you are a creative person, from developing your story in your unique way. So don't plan on regurgitating some other writer's story. It won't work, and readers will label you as a fake or a fraud, and will despise you for ever. And I am sure you won't want that label. Your writing career will have a very short life.

So tell a story. Tell your story. Make sure yours really is a story that must be told. Then tell it.

When you have created the plot, the characters, the setting, and decided that yours really is that great story that has to be told, then it is probably the right time to sit down and begin writing it.

All stories follow a similar format, but never let your editor or publisher know that you are writing to a formula. The formula basically tells us that you have those ingredients that we have mentioned already — setting, characters, plot. But all stories must have a beginning. The beginning can't just drift into some narrative. It must be a beginning to the life situation you are about to unfold for your readers. All fiction must have a conflict. How boring would it be if nothing happened? And your readers will want a sound resolution, or climax. Don't leave them up in the air wondering if the character really went to Spain, or stayed at home to cause more disturbances to the household, or ended their life in jail. Readers will want to be satisfied that what you did with all those people in the end was in keeping with their expectations.

So you still want to be a writer? Having all those good ideas is not going to get you very far. If they are in your head, they will be inaccessible until they are released. And the only way you can release them is to tell those stories. One story already told is far better than a thousand good ideas you would one day like to write about if you get around to it.

It will only be when you have finished each story, when it is written, polished, made to shine, that the story really comes to life. It is only then that you will be able to share it with your readers, and declare yourself to be a writer.

When writing fiction—your story—you will need to start with an idea. But that is good because ideas are everywhere you care to look for them. Look around you for that special piece of inspiration. Life is full of characters, especially when you create characters based on all sorts of people you meet in everyday life.

Listen in to other people's conversations. They could be full of plots, sub-plots, and everything else you could care to weave into your story. Why are those two people whispering? What is their secret? You can't hear what they are saying? That doesn't matter. Make it up to suit your story. Think about what they could be saying.

Look all around you. Look at the other people in your life—those you work with, those you ride home with on the bus or the train. Put some action into their thoughts. What! You don't know what they are planning? Then think about some of the things that could be going through their minds. Be creative. There is no limit to how creative you can become when you write fiction. You just have to write that story that is special, is different, and so engaging that your readers will want to finish the story right to the end.

Let's look at the elements of a story, such as a novel.

Nothing happens at random. There can never be dead ends in fiction. If something happens, then it must happen for a reason. If someone leaves a story, even momentarily, then they will leave it for a good reason. If a character appears, the person is present for a reason. If he or she has no reason to be there, then delete them.

Just as happens in real life, we all have our own agendas. So too in our story. Each character will have a different agenda for themselves. With good writing, it is your job to bring those agendas together in a masterful way so the collection of all those agendas becomes a whole.

THE PLOT

A story will have a plot. This is the interesting part of a story. It's the part that puts the characters together, and where they act and react to one another for whatever reason you have given them. It's the plot that makes the story interesting. A short story can only have one plot, while a novel can have several sub-plots that are bought together in the final resolution. If all those sub-plots are not brought together, with one or two just conveniently forgotten, then they must be eliminated. A good plot is merely the skeleton of the story on which you will hang your characters, and tie in all the other components of your story. On its own, a plot is nothing. It will fail. It needs the muscles of the body to hold the bones together, and to make it work, and to make it move forward.

Those characters talk to each other. Or, if they are not talking to each other, then there should be a very good reason for their silence. Show what that reason is if there is no communication between the characters. That could be the very reason why you are telling the story.

Dialogue can really make a good story successful. Poor dialogue can kill off an otherwise good story. If dialogue is hard to follow, is boring, unnecessary, then this type of conversation is not going to do much to make the other characters happy, and your readers won't be impressed with you for making them waste their time reading a lot of unnecessary drivel. Each character should say only what needs to be said to move the story forward.

Your characters will need to be involved in a conflict of some sort. A conflict does not need to be a major battle or a war going on somewhere. It can be two people who have to resolve an issue together, or one person to resolve their fight with their inner demons at the expense and the suffering of the other person. A conflict can be as complicated as you wish to make it. As long as it is feasible, and sounds logical and reasonable to the reader, there is no reason why you can't have the conflict that you impose on your characters.

SETTING
Setting. Where's your story set? Which country? Which city? In an office? In a house? The detailed description of setting, built up gradually, is essential. Readers want to know where your story is taking place, and in what period. Is it this century? Or perhaps was it set in the 1800s in London?

DON'T MAKE YOUR STORY TOO PREDICTABLE
Don't make your story predictable. If you do, then you have given your reader no reason at all to read it. He would have every reason to ask—why did he waste his time reading it, and why did you waste your time writing it? If your readers guess the ending right at the start, then you are not offering them very much, are you?

Although you must never let your readers guess the ending too early, every element you introduce must have been foreseen. You can't have someone with the amazing ability to go across a canyon on a tightrope if you have not given your readers some clue that he has performed similar amazing feats of courage in a circus, or in his job of climbing to the tops of the giant redwoods in America to rescue cats that have been dumb enough to climb to the top of the trees and can't find their way down. If you get your character to do anything amazing, then this feat should be within their realistic and identified capacity to do so, unless it is the story of a person who is plunged into heroic acts to save his loved ones or his family pet from a fire. That action could reasonably be within his makeup.

POINT OF VIEW

Who is going to tell the story?

Three points of view are commonly used.

The first is the first person single — 'I saw him climb the wall and he disappeared. I looked over the wall and saw what he was up to.' Here, the narrator is probably one of the characters, possibly the main character.

The second point of view is the objective point of view. This is used when the writer tells the reader what happens without stating more than can be gleaned from the dialogue or from the action. The one telling the story never discloses anything about the pending action or about the characters and how they think or feel, because he can't possibly know these things. The narrator of a story in which the objective point of view is used is always detached from the reader. Here, using the objective point of view, the narrator is never a character.

The most popular point of view through which to tell a story is through the third person. The story is told in the past tense ' ... he then scaled the wall and slid down the other side ...' Here, the one telling the story is not one of the characters, and is in no way part of the story.

CHARACTERS

Before you even begin to write your story, consider your characters. How many will you need to tell your story, and who are they, and what are they?

Once you have identified your characters you will need to consider where you are going to place them. Make sure that the setting you decide on fits the part for the characters. It might be necessary to change a character or two to make them fit into the story better. It might even be necessary to change the setting so that you can keep those delightful characters you have created, but put them somewhere else for now so they can mess around, play up, cause all sorts of mischief if that's what you had in mind.

Your characters can be anyone you like. They could be based on real people. They could be imaginary folks from a run-down and neglected village. One aspect that many writers enjoy about fiction is that they can make their characters do everything they want them to do. They can make them violent, kind, intelligent, they can turn nice people into criminals, and they can turn criminals into really nice people. Try doing all that in real life!

Your characters, whether based on real people or not, will all have the same characteristics to a point. They will live, they will breathe. They will speak just like real people, they will hold discussions with others in your story. They can be modern people, or old fashioned individuals who don't fit into the modern world of young people. How would you like to see all your characters in your work of fiction? Are they sexy, always womanising the opposite sex? Are they vibrant, go-getters, the achievers? Or are they always trying to take something from those who get in their way? They are your characters, so make them as you want them to be.

When you create characters, they must fit the role you have in mind for them to play. The wrong person in the wrong setting at the wrong time will not work, and you will struggle to finish your story. Bringing awkward people into line and constantly having to round them up and bring them back into their place will be very tiring for you and awkward for your readers.

Create people who fit the role you have created for them. It's your story you are telling, so create the people in it that you like to work with.

Now develop those characters. Give them shape. Give them a personality. Give them a life of their own. Think about every aspect of them that you can — what they do for work, their education background, their likes and dislikes, their personalities, whether they are emotional people or cold swines. Are they large or small? Thin or obese? Intelligent or not? You may not need to include all this information in your story, but if you know your characters well, then you can work with them and make them do whatever you want them to do for you. By knowing them well, you can't spring any surprises on your readers when they do something out of character. You should be able to predict their behaviour, and make them behave according to the image you have created for each of them.

Characters are easy to create, but it is not so easy to create just the right character to fill the role you have in mind.

Go shopping and stand in a queue. Look at the people in front of you at the checkout. Put some personality into that person. Think about the type of person they could really be. Would you like to meet them? Why? Why not? Do they look cruel? Then they might be just the person you want to fill that important role. Think of all those creeps and the sociopaths you have had the misfortune to work with over the years. Seek revenge! Turn them into evil monsters in your story.

The personality of your characters is generally brought out for the readers' benefit through their actions, and through their dialogue.

Try to create characters who are different from each other. If there is a very good reason why two or more characters should be similar, that's fine as long as you can justify their similarities. But in real life, we have a whole mixture of different people, with different personalities, and different reasons for living. So too with good fiction the characters would be mixed up, they should be different so there is conflict that needs to be resolved in the following pages.

The characters you create should at least be plausible. This is critical to good storytelling. But believable does not mean they should fit a mould. They can be weak, but plausible. They can be strong, but plausible. They can be any way you want to create them, but make them seem real, and human if that is the theme of your story.

Characters can be turned into individuals by simple actions on the writers' part. Dress him or her in a different outfit, and watch their personality change. Let him change jobs, and watch the difference. Let her change her opinions, and you have changed your character. Change the person's inner feelings towards their partner, and again you will see a different person emerging. Give them something interesting to say, and that in turn will become more interesting. That's how easy it can be to create your ideal character for that special occasion. Create the character you want, the one who is going to fit in with the rest of the story you are creating, and he will do all the things that you tell him to do. Readers really have to believe the character would do just what you have made him do. If the readers can't believe that his actions would be plausible, then they won't believe the rest of the story either.

Create the most suitable character for your story. It's like sending people for a job interview. Only the one most suitable will be selected for the job. So too only those most suitable characters should be selected for the job of making your story work. Determine each character's part, whether major or minor, and their involvement with each other, and their importance in the story.

DIALOGUE

Dialogue is important. Good dialogue tells the reader about the moods of your characters, and about their emotions. It tells the reader how those two people interact, or react to each other. It tells the reader more about the story, and helps to move the story along a bit.

Dialogue is reacting to what each one says. That way, dialogue flows smoothly. There must be a reason for the second response to the first person's speech. He or she reacts to what is said, and to the way it is said. Dialogue should never be independent of the story, but should be integrated into the whole story. Make each character react, and include other characters who react to each of those characters. You can create a real storm if several characters react to what is being said, depending on the way it is said. The response of one character to another should be in keeping with the story, and must be in keeping with the personality of the character. If one character is on edge all the time, then their reaction to what is said would be different from that of another character who was so calm that he became sickening because he accepted everything that life served up to him and was happy with that.

Creating dialogue should be no more difficult than creating the ideal character, or characters, for your story. Put your character in front of a mirror and get him to say something. What is the likely reaction he could expect? How would he respond to that person's remark? What would be the subsequent response? Could another character add his few cents worth to the debate? Now you have two others responding to each other.

Dialogue should sound like real speech. It is difficult to listen to a person who is not speaking properly. It is even harder to read what someone has said if they are not coherent and clear. The reader of any story does not want to bother trying to work out what the character might have said, could have said, and wonder why they didn't say something a bit more realistic. And just like in real life where we are insulted when people talk rubbish to us, your characters should not say things that are rubbish either. If they did, it's your readers who have their intelligence insulted. And you certainly don't want to do that.

In dialogue, you can convey a lot of information to your readers. It's not just about responding to another person. Make each piece of dialogue move the story forward. Impart important information about almost everything through dialogue. Develop setting through dialogue. Use dialogue to develop your characters, and bring out some of their important traits however you can through what they say and the way they say it. If you can develop the story this way, that's a lot easier than including long descriptive pieces about setting or about each character.

Don't make a character say something merely to fill a space. We don't like the bores of life who say plenty when they have nothing much to say, and neither do your readers. So make sure that whatever your characters say really is important to the story's development.

With dialogue that is written well, it should not be necessary to tell your readers that the person was angry. 'Don't do that! I have told you before!' tells your reader that he is angry, and is rather tired of repeating himself.

'I'm cold,' she complained bitterly. 'I'm always cold.'

'I'll light the fire.'

'Don't do that. Last time you lit the fire you made the room smoky.'

'That was last time. I'll be careful this time.'

'Don't bother. I'll do it myself.'

From this short piece of dialogue, we soon get the impression that 'she' is unhappy, she is bad tempered, that 'he' can't do anything right, she likes to have something to complain about, and probably, their relationship is not very strong. Perhaps it might even be time for the couple to move on in their own ways! With dialogue, show, don't tell. Let your readers use their imagination, and earn their enjoyment while reading your story.

Don't make one character go on and on and on for several pages. If you need large pieces of dialogue, break it up with interjections, with descriptions, with a knock on the door, the telephone ringing and so on. Large blocks of dialogue can be boring, as it comes from only one point of view. This is especially hard for your readers to take when they know there are other characters present who would like to contribute to the conversation if they could ever get a word in.

YOUR STYLE. YOUR STORY

You will personalise your story by developing your own style. This is merely the way in which you tell your story. It's the way you write, the way you describe the action, and the descriptions of the setting and of the characters. It's your use of long and short sentences, and long and short paragraphs. It's the use of many short chapters, or the use of several very long chapters. Style is really you, telling your story, your way.

Style is what you do with the story you have written. Good storytelling style does not require that every rule of grammar should be perfectly followed. Put in some deliberate imperfections from time to time, but make sure they look as if they were deliberate, and not just your carelessness coming through your writing. It's often the little things ... the way things are said ... how things are ... that make interesting writing. Aim for perfection with your writing, but don't aim for perfection with the rules of grammar.

Can you speak Italian? Or German? Possibly, but many of your readers can't speak anything other than English, and foreign phrases would be wasted on them. Worse still, the readers would be annoyed with you if they had slabs of a foreign language that they could not understand. Why would they even try to understand? It's not smart to confuse your reader. Be smarter than that!

If all sentences were to be only twelve words long, can you imagine how boring your writing would be? Every sentence the same as the previous one. Every sentence following would be just the same length. And no doubt every paragraph would consist of five or six sentences.

Good writing entails more than consistency. Good writing, and good style, require inconsistencies, and lots and lots of them.

Vary the lengths of each sentence. Make some long. Others, short.

KEEP THE STORY FRESH

Freshness is important in your story, so keep it fresh at all times. Imagine going to the supermarket to buy vegetables that you saw there two weeks ago, and each visit since then. You would be turned right off. It's the same with writing. Good writing is fresh writing, with fresh, original ideas. Your ideas. Aim for far more than a boring public-service style of writing, where there is no originality, no creativity showing, and no reader response either.

WRITING YOUR STORY

Isn't it time we got down to writing the story you have always wanted to tell?

Then start with the first paragraph. This is the one that is going to help readers decide if the story is worth their time in continuing with it. If the first paragraph is dull, they might extend themselves to the second, maybe—only maybe—the third paragraph. After that, they will put the book away and walk out of the shop without buying a copy, and you will have defeated the purpose of writing the story.

In that first paragraph, you could introduce the main character, or hint at his imminent arrival. You could give a brief description of the setting too, so readers can imaging where the story is at least going to start. But don't give too much away. Build up the characters, build up the plot, build up the setting and build up the conflict bit by bit as you progress further. Don't tell your readers everything at the beginning.

What kind of story are you telling? Readers will have in their minds the type of story it is likely to be. So don't disappoint them. If you intend the story to be humorous, then keep the funny bits coming. But make sure they really are funny, not just to you, but to others as well. Don't create a half-and-half story, where part is romance, and the second half is sad. You can introduce grief into a romance or to a serious account, but only as long as the grief is appropriate and is intended.

In the beginning, show your main character under some kind of stress if that is what the story is about. Hint at the other characters who will enter the story. You could hint that Uncle Barnaby is about to arrive and bring his venom and spread that wherever he goes. He doesn't have to be there in the opening paragraph.

Tell your story through actions and through dialogue, not through long blocks of narrative. There should be no surprises, although in fiction, it is the unexpected that makes for interesting storytelling.

All action should have a reason. What is the reason for the action you are introducing in your story?

You can develop the main plot as a series of sub-plots, these are eventually interwoven and they come together and fit perfectly into place in the end. That keeps the action alive, and the story moving forward. Just what your reader is looking for!

If your main character has options that he could pursue, this could make the story interesting for your readers. Let the character take the wrong action, and follow the route that is different from the obvious one, and is not the path readers would have chosen. But if you make the character take a different path, make sure everything turns out right for him in the end. That does not mean that all results have to be perfect from that moment. He might have to take evasive action and come out on top in the action, but that is acceptable as long as the reader is asking questions — why did he do that? Why didn't he do what I told him to do? Oh, I see, he was able to correct his mistake and come out on top anyway.

RE-WRITING YOUR STORY

When you have finished your story, you will need to edit it heavily, and possibly rewrite much of it. Accept that as part of the writing process. If you have to tidy up the whole manuscript, then you can be assured that the result will be much better the second time around. And if, after the revision you are still not happy with it, then rewrite the whole manuscript a third time. If you are not happy with it, your readers will not like it, and the publisher won't like it either.

Did every action have a purpose? If not, take it out. Be prepared to revise it, to rewrite it until you can't remove a single word more, or shorten one more sentence.

Create a good story the editor or publisher enjoys, and you can be pretty sure that your readers will enjoy your creativity too. Who can tell where your writing and your talents will take you?

For many writers, the writing part is the easy stage in the whole process. For them, it's a matter of outlining the work they want to write, putting a lot of words down on paper (or these days, on their computers and more likely, on their tablets or mobile phones) and then editing the result. The editing means rewriting, rewriting, and then rewriting some more until not a single word looks out of place, says everything that the writer wanted it to say, and then they can put it aside feeling satisfied that the result is a good story.

With all writing, including creative writing, or fiction, rewriting is the one most important ingredient of the whole writing process. Let me say that again. For all writing, rewriting is the most important ingredient of the whole writing process.

If you finish writing the first draft and on re-reading it you feel that you could have said things a lot better, then get to work and make them better. It won't hurt you, it will take time, but it will, or should, turn you from being a very mediocre writer to one who is considered by readers as a good writer, or even a great writer.

Chapter 5 The Romance Novel

Everyone loves a romance (well, most people do). They like to see a couple happy, close together in their relationship, everything going well for them, and both partners becoming successful in life, and achieving everything they set out to do together.

Unfortunately, life's not like that very often. And even if we were to find that 'perfect couple', wouldn't the story be boring? Boy meets girl, they fall in love, live happily ever afterwards, end of story. Zzzzzzzzz. How boring is that?

We feel warm inside when we see that couple walking along the banks of the river holding hands, or the couple on the park bench, she, her head on his shoulder, he with his arm around her. We love that. To a certain extent. Too much of it and it becomes almost sickening. Why aren't our own lives like that? Why would they live in a perfect world while we struggle with everyone in our own lives? And why should we have to go through hell and back again in our relationships to even survive? How dare someone have that perfect relationship.

BE A STORYTELLER

A good romantic story begins with a genuine and honest love of telling a story. Be a storyteller, but make sure you are a good storyteller. And make it a story that you really want to tell. It will read so much more easily and it will be much easier for you to write it.

You might consider starting by reading several romances in the style that you like to get a feel for what is required, what's needed to put together that great romance you are about to start writing. Always remember — it really could be that great romance!

You will need a fresh and original approach. Don't imitate the characters of another storyteller. Don't even try to copy some other storyteller's plot. It will show that you are not being honest with your readers. It's your story, so everything — story, characters, style — must be your own. Anyway, if you try putting someone else's characters into your own plot, the story will most likely collapse in a heap of paper in the recycle bin.

For a good romantic story to succeed, you must be part of the story. I don't mean that you should be one of the characters. I mean that you should feel so passionately about the story you are telling that the story will become part of you. If you remain distant from the characters and from the action, then the story will lose a lot of that intimate closeness readers expect.

Your story must hold the interest of your readers from the first page. You must think of that really great opening paragraph. On reflection, make that the first sentence. If your beginning of the story does nothing for the reader, then consider that person as a reader, or worse still, a publisher, you have just lost. So the first sentence should grab the reader's attention. The first paragraph will complete that stage of getting their attention and holding it until the resolution at the end of the book.

In your opening, you should make a point of revealing your own individual touch, so readers realise that you are a new author, not a rehash of one they did not even like. With a little thought, you can bring out your individuality, and your fresh and individual approach to storytelling early in the novel or story.

You will need to give a lot of thought to your characters. You won't need a lot of main characters—just enough to carry the story along in a planned way so the reader is satisfied. Don't include one extra character who does not serve a vital role in your story. There is no room in stories for characters who do not belong there, even if you like them. So if you like them, give them something to do that is worth their while.

YOU NEED A PLAN

In any relationship, it is pretty safe to say that it is, or has been, far from perfect since day one.

Consider other people. Look at their backgrounds. Look at the demons they have to live with in their own lives. Think of the conflicts that enter and leave their lives. Or, worse still, think of the conflicts that come into a person's life, and they stay there, despite the person's best efforts to eradicate them.

We all have those demons within that are going to throw out all our best plans, turn good to nasty, good to evil, happiness to sadness.

With a typical couple, he, on the surface, could give the appearances of a well-adjusted, mature individual, getting to where he has always wanted to go. But think of how he would be feeling if he has been fighting sexual abuse by the priests at his school while he was a small boy. That infliction will be with him for the rest of his life, undermining his relationship with a girl.

Or he might have had an alcoholic father. That's enough to upset any person, no matter how mature and well adjusted they might seem on the surface.

Or his parents might have moved from house to house every few months for no apparent reason. He thinks that is the way life should be.

We all react to our backgrounds, and indeed we usually find that something that happened to us as a child could still be exerting a strong influence on our thinking, on our development (or lack of personal development). We might find that attitudes we succumbed to as teenagers could well explain our attitudes to children, to work, to women, to violence, many, many years after the original incidents were forgotten. Our minds try to fade out the undesirable fields in our lives, but their influences can still remain for many years. Just ask any psychologist about the trauma they must share with those people they work with.

How different every couple is, and how different every individual in any relationship is.

We have to consider the characters in our story as individuals. Look at their circumstances. Then we have to put those two people, with all their backgrounds, together to make a life together as one.

That's the challenge you will be facing if you want to write romance.

Like any fiction, a romance must have those same ingredients of any other fiction: plot, conflict, setting, and, most importantly, characters who interact with each other. And we must have resolution of that conflict — how they resolve their problems and come together in the end.

In real life, it is more than likely that the girl will have more than one male chasing after her. If she has all the qualities you have given your heroine, it is unlikely she would be alone in the world for very long. If she is everything you could imagine a perfect heroine to be, then she won't be the type to wait around for Mr Average to show up and take her away. Mr Average would have to act very quickly if he were to capture the attention of someone who stood out this much.

It will only happen after they have sorted out their differences, conquered their inner demons. They will then be able live not only with each other, but just as importantly, will be able to live with themselves. Then, and only then, will we be able to draw the story to a satisfactory conclusion. The readers will be satisfied that the characters have been through enough turmoil. At last they got on top of their problems and are able to get on as they had hoped they would from page one of our romantic novel. Where do you start writing a romantic novel?

DEVELOP YOUR PLAN
How are you going to plan your story?

Grab some sheets of paper and a good pen!

On the first page, write out the general outline of the whole story — don't go into too much detail at this stage — that will come on subsequent pages.

Now, on each of the other sheets of paper, put the number of the chapter at the top, with the working title of each chapter. The title of the chapters does not appear on the final manuscript, but by adding these at this stage, you will be able to see clearly what action goes into each chapter.

Now fill in the details of your story, chapter by chapter. Allocate a set amount of space for each piece of action, for setting, and for the action component of your story.

As you get into writing your story, you will most likely find that the story takes on a different direction, with perhaps a different slant from the one you originally planned. That is alright, just let it happen. You will feel happier with the new direction if that's the way the story was to head anyway, so don't try to force it back on track at this stage. Leave it. You can always use the original plan for story two.

You should try to build mystery into the story all the way through to keep the readers guessing, and to remain interested in your story. If there's no underlying intrigue, how are you going to get your readers to appreciate the couple's struggles? You will have the main story, but intermingled with the main story, you will have subtle sub-plots that carry the story forward between the main events until the hero and heroine come back together again at the end.

Develop your characters. List them, one each on a new sheet of paper. Here, you should include everything about them, even, at the risk of sounding facetious, what they had for breakfast. Unless you know your main characters intimately, you won't be able to make them behave as you want them to. And if they don't do what you want of them, or expect of them, you will find your story going off in different directions. Your characters will hold the story together, they will drive it forward, and they will even make it work for you. So know your characters, and make them behave according to your rules, not theirs.

THE PLOT

The plot will be the next ingredient of the story you will have to address. What happens? Why? What does each action and sub-plot mean? Is each incident important? If it is, it needs to be included. If it's not important, leave it out of this story and include it in the next story you write.

In this part of the story, include as much of the proposed action as you can — the meetings, their significance, the emotions they evoke, feelings each character will experience on meeting the other characters, how they relate to your setting. If emotions change, or are likely to change, you will need to tell your readers this, and tell them too why the feelings and emotions of each character changed. This is important. That's how life is. In fact, the reason why emotions change through the story is probably the reason for the story in the first place. So expect people to change as you develop them, because that's human nature.

CONFLICT

What conflict are you going to introduce? What is the main thing going to be that will need resolution? It has to be a strong conflict, requiring a dramatic resolution. That's one of the main ingredients that is going to carry the story forward. So make the conflict strong, but make sure the resolution matches the intensity of the conflict. You don't want a strong conflict that is going to change everything around the main characters, with a resolution so weak the readers are going to be left wondering about what really happened. In other words, how did the story end? Hopefully, it will end on a happy note.

In far too many relationships, we encounter people who are always trying to antagonise their partner, often in a vicious way. They complain about their friends, they complain about the dog the woman bought. They complain loudly about ... well, they just complain, and stir up animosity, and become disrespectful of their partner. They try hard to be antagonistic, and usually succeed. Your readers might, unfortunately, already have a life-form of this nature in her life (yes, males are the ones who fit this category most often). They won't want to read about yet another person they don't want in their life, even if that person is there only in a temporary capacity in the book they are reading.

DON'T INCLUDE VIOLENCE OR BELITTLING
Topical subjects are usually okay, but one that has never been accepted in romance fiction is domestic violence.

Many people are subjected to that atrocity in their own lives, and they certainly don't want to read about it. So don't even contemplate it. And constantly putting others down, something that occurs too frequently in the real world, is certainly not acceptable either.

Violence of any form is a definite no-no. Your strong hero should show admirable self control at all times, even if he were to be driven to the point where any of us would give in and react to those forces around us. For some readers, it might ring too much like their own lives that they are trying to escape from by reading romance. They want the opposite, but the hero can nevertheless be a strong type — without resorting to violence.

Unfortunately, this is conflict in the real world, but luckily, this type of conflict could be left out of a romance. Otherwise ... it just wouldn't be a romance, would it?

In the conflict, you can have incidents that keep the lovers apart, always craving to be in each other's arms. So why aren't they together? I know that you will probably want to say that if you brought them together, the story would end, and so it would. But tell your readers why they can't come together, give readers at least a glimmer of hope that before too long, they will be living as one. That's what they want to read, so make sure you write the story with your readers in mind.

SUB-PLOTS

Within each major conflict there will always be minor skirmishes, small conflicts that will need some sort of resolution on a lesser scale than will be needed to reach the final climax of the story. Each conflict will have to be dealt with, but not necessarily as soon as it arises. It is alright, in a well-written story, to resolve minor issues progressively throughout the book. Think about your real-life situation. If a problem develops this afternoon, it might not always be possible to fix things on the spot. There will be residual bits and pieces that you will still need to sort out, and often some of the small issues will influence one another and have an impact on issues further through the week or month.

In your plan, decide where each conflict arises, and where in your story you are going to place the resolution to each little romantic mess-up.

With any major conflict, we all show inner emotions that are not always apparent to those we talk to, or to those we work with or to others in our lives. Those inner conflicts could also be what the whole story is about. If their inner feelings are significant to the outcome, tell your readers how the heroine feels, why she feels that way, what she could do about it, and what she has done to help herself overcome her sadness up to now. But of course you will weave the story around all these inner feelings and inner conflicts. You won't resolve them on the next page, in one or two paragraphs—more likely the rest of the story will be needed to resolve everything satisfactorily. And by that I mean satisfactorily to the heroine, and also satisfactorily to the readers. Don't leave your heroine dangling, while at the same time you leave you readers wondering what happened.

CREATING YOUR CHARACTERS

With romance, it is the characters that make the story more than anything else. So you will have to create characters who are just ideal for the story you have in mind. Remember that a character you created for a different story might not fit the one you are writing now. So create individual characters who are really part of the current story.

You must—and I can't emphasise this point enough—build a character profile of each main character. Write down everything you can think of that pertains to him or to her, including his physical build, his complexion, his hair style, mannerisms, speech and so on. If police were interviewing a witness, they would be seeking this same information. You will need to provide yourself with all the same details, down to the last dimple and last slur of speech.

Your apparent description should be made in no more than the first two or three chapters. If you don't reveal the person's full personality or characteristics, your readers will be in for quite a surprise when your hero or heroine does something unexpected of them. And that is a sign of bad writing!

Who is your hero? What is he like? What does he do for a living? Is he honest? Is he sincere—is that part of the conflict? Is he likeable? If not, then how did the girl first show any interest in him? If he is likeable, why hasn't someone else already run off with him? If someone else were to be interested in him because of his charms and everything else you can put into this one person, then quite likely your story would have a different storyline and a completely different ending.

Your characters should appear real. They will be individuals, but they must, to your readers, appear real. They must be strong enough to be able to convince your readers that the person is a real human being. The readers must be able to relate to each character. Their actions, their dialogue, their motives must be sincere. Unless, of course, the whole story is based on a person who is not at all sincere, and that is what causes the conflict with the other person in the relationship. That insincerity must be made a strong point throughout your story, and should be conveyed to the readers so that, in their minds, they can see clearly how the person's insincerity is the cause of the conflict and that is the point of the story, and the issue they both have to address.

If your hero is supposed to be strong, then his actions should be those of a person of strong character. If he is supposed to be one in authority wherever he goes, then people should be able to look up to him. If he is not a strong person, then his actions and his dialogue should reflect the person he is. Other characters in your story should react in an appropriate way to that person.

Occupations and professional backgrounds of your main characters are very important. In similar situations, a chef is likely to react differently to a political activist, or to a corporate director. So if your heroine is the director of her own multinational company, tell your readers about her role in her position – about how she came to be in that position, how she developed her business, how she became so successful. Remember today that many women are extremely successful and competent business owners. It is not exaggerating to say that many such women are millionaires in their own right without the influence of any hero in their lives. If your heroine is a real achiever, give her credit for her achievements, because she deserves it.

Your chosen characters should be able to fit into their environment. Unless, of course, the conflict arises when one or more of your characters behaves in a certain way because they don't belong in the city you have placed them. If that happens, you might have to move them to an area they can relate to, and one where they belong. Or, if they are deliberately out of place, help them resolve their problem of being in the wrong place. Conflict often arises by a person being in the wrong place at the wrong possible time.

In a really sound relationship, each person must remain interested in the other one. At the same time, each person in that relationship must remain interesting to the other one. How is your heroine going to remain interesting to her hero? How is she going to stand out from everyone else and be that bright light in his otherwise dull day? And what is your hero going to do each day to make himself shine so that she can admire his full personality and character? Sorry, but taking an endless series of selfies and putting drivel on Facebook at every opportunity won't count for much in this regard, or in any other meaningful way.

If I wanted to meet a new heroine in my life, I would want to meet someone who inspires others through her talents, through her skills, or her involvement in the things that she is doing in her everyday life—perhaps the very reason why we are unable to be together for the duration of our story, or our life. What is your hero going to do to be an inspiration to those in his world? He must stand out from the crowd if she is ever going to notice him. My new heroine certainly wouldn't want to know me if I came home each evening from a boring job pushing a pen around a desk all day long, and then sat in front of the television set for three hours each evening. I am sure the new heroine in my life would be waving goodbye to me very soon if I dared to live a life so mundane as that.

Just as in the real world, many people find everything just so much of a bother. There's no point to doing anything, so why should I bother with ... I am sure you have encountered such people. Your readers don't want to read about such boring people. Your hero must be someone with get up and go, and should be getting on with the job with the minimum amount of noise, disregarding the criticism of those around him. He knows his place in the world, he knows where he belongs, and gets there with the least amount of complaints. These are the people that heroes are made of in the real world, just as they should be the types that become heroes in fiction.

USING DIALOGUE

Dialogue is another important ingredient of a story, particularly in a romantic story. Dialogue does more than just convey feelings. It can be used to carry the story along quite well on its own. If a girl shouted at her lover, then you don't need to tell your reader that she was angry. It would be obvious that she was angry. And if she were to tell him that she only had twenty dollars to buy food for the week, you don't need to tell your readers that they were poor, and that she is blaming him for his inadequacy of not being able to provide for her as he had promised before they got together. Dialogue is so important also in setting mood, conveying information, giving readers an insight into possible action that could be just around the corner.

There are many, many people in the real world who have plenty to say about everything. They take half an hour to complain that the coffee isn't really hot. Luckily, your readers will be spared from characters like this, because in all writing, you don't have the luxury of using many words to say nothing. Anyway, you wouldn't have any readers left either if your hero or heroine carried on like that—it's rather childish behaviour at the best of times, and very irritating. Don't annoy your readers.

Does the hero's comment evoke anger? Why? How does she respond to that remark she took the wrong way? If he didn't intend her to take it the wrong way, then what did he mean by it? Have one react to the other in a two-way approach.

Dialogue is not just two people talking. It is two or more people reacting. Listen to conversation—either with your own friends or partner, those you work with, or even if you overhear a conversation. Person one will say something—it might be a wish, or a statement. Person two responds to that comment. And then person one responds to that person's comment, until a whole conversation, or dialogue, is built up.

Dialogue should fit the person saying it. Don't make dialogue out of character, because if you do, then your character will not work. The dialogue is part of that person, so what that person says, and also the way that person says it, should fit his personality profile.

Good dialogue has several functions:

- To tell us, through the conversations of the characters, what we need to know to make sense of the story;
- It conveys character: to show us what kinds of people we are dealing with;

- It conveys a sense of place and time: to evoke the speech patterns, vocabulary and rhythms of specific kinds of people;
- To develop conflict: to dominate others, or to interact with others.

Good dialogue depends on making it as natural as possible. Conversation is not generally grammatically perfect. It is full of ums and ers and other irritations the listeners become used to. Sentences are often left incomplete. However, if you 'write as it is spoke', you won't have many readers finishing your stories. They will lose interest after the fourth um and second er and the fifth pause. Find the balance between written English and conversational English. Know your characters. Know what they would say and how they would say it. Listen to people around you speaking. I mean really listen to them. Sometimes in conversation, we don't even finish sentences. In writing, it is alright to leave sentences unfinished ... to a point.

SETTING

Where's your story taking place? Ah, I can hear you saying now. Anywhere I want it to happen. You are right to a point, because with good writing, you could have your hero and heroine circling the world three times looking for happiness. But they are more likely to find it in one place, perhaps a short distance from one another but not so close they are brought together too quickly.

But pick your location well, keeping in mind your characters. Different characters probably belong better to some locations and some situations than others. And often with a good story, location determines outcome. It can determine behaviour. Behaviour determines the resolution of the whole conflict. So pick a setting you can relate to, one you know well, so that if you have them walking along the street holding hands, you can identify the actual street they are walking along at any time. That's how well you need to know your setting. Don't just tell the readers the couple walked along the street. That won't mean much. Describe the shops. Describe the river. Describe the people in the street. What are they wearing? Are they middle class? Are they ruffians? Are they dressed in suites and ties? Are they casual? Time of day will be important, so describe the sunshine on the couple, because sunshine will hint that it is set in daytime in one of the warmer months. Include all these details in your plan.

A good story can move from one area to another, from one country to another, but it can't take place just anywhere, or, worse still, nowhere. It must have a physical location, real or imaginary. An imaginary location, such as a particular house, within a city, is fine. But remember these days, a lot of your readers would have travelled far, and if you identify a particular house, a particular building on a particular street in a particular city, it is more than likely at least one of your readers would have been to that city, know that building well because they grew up there, and then complain that it is nothing like the house you described. Your story then begins to lose credibility. The rest of the story will be treated with contempt, or more possibly, the readers won't even be interested in finishing reading it.

If you transport your characters to a foreign location, perhaps in an attempt to help them resolve their difficulties, then you must know something—indeed a lot—about that new location. Don't send them to Paris if you have never been to Paris. Don't send them off to live in a small rural village if you have never been outside the city. Other readers would have lived in the country, and they would realise that a country lifestyle is just so different from city life. So make sure you have spent at least some time not only in the location you first place your story, but if you move it out of that area, make sure you know the new location intimately.

If you move the characters and the story off-shore, this can introduce new conflicts too. If this is what you intend doing with your story, that is fine. But remember that in a foreign land, the characters will be facing isolation. That isolation will come from being distant from their own family and friends. They will know no one there. They will have no friends until they settle in, and that might take a considerable time. You could have a language barrier that makes the main characters even more isolated. If they can't speak the language of their new location, they can't fit in.

In a foreign land, what prospects are there for each character to find work? Not being proficient in the language could prevent either of them, or both of them, from finding meaningful employment. Again, you are introducing another conflict. If this was your intention, that's fine, and you can work out a resolution to this latest crisis that arises in the lives of your characters. But if this was not what you intended when you moved them offshore or even into a new locality, then it just won't work.

Don't expect to move your characters to some remote colony in Africa and expect all the people in that locality to speak fluent English. Some will. Most won't. The language barrier will lead to further isolation and conflict.

OCCUPATIONS

With your characters, you will have determined the occupations for each of them. They must do something. Know how that occupation fits into the real world. If you place your heroine in a scientific laboratory where she gets a lot of mental stimulation from her work and from her work colleagues, then you should know what a scientific laboratory is all about, what it does, and how it works. And this is something you cannot get a proper feel for merely by reading about life in a laboratory. You will have had to spend time in one yourself.

Keep your occupations, and the work environment of your characters, familiar to you. After all, you have to convey that information to your readers who may not have had the pleasure (dubious or real) of having served on the board of a corporation, or worked in a laboratory where experiments are carried out that you, or your readers, may not agree with, such as using animals for testing of new products, or in the name of scientific research. You must know the reasons for all the actions, and the thinking of the people around your characters, and be able to explain why they did such and such, in keeping with the actions and thoughts and ethics of those around them.

If your hero is on the board of a huge corporation (the very thing that has led to his wealth) then you will need to know what life is like for serving members of boards of huge corporations.

It is alright to describe the character's main attributes, but not at the expense of slowing down the story. If you slow down the beginning of the story too much by including excessive amounts of personal description, you might lose your readers. Physical descriptions such as appearance and personality descriptions should be woven into the story as much as possible, perhaps describing a trait by action more than anything. That keeps the story moving forward at a steady pace, while at the same time imparting a lot of information.

MIXED CULTURES
Something that has changed in recent years in fiction, just as it has in real life, is the mixed cultures in relationships. Years ago, boy would meet girl from the same area and fall in love. Now, in real life, and it shouldn't be any different in fiction, because fiction in many ways copies real life, one person could come from America, live in South-East Asia, and while on a trip in Australia, meet a girl from the Middle East. Here, you as an author will have different issues to deal with in your story. Those cultures could be the cause of much conflict (or at least you can make them to appear so even if they wouldn't exist in the real world).

If you include mixed cultures, you must at all times respect those cultures and those customs in the country to which you have transported your characters.

A word of caution is essential here. The only way you can fully understand and appreciate other cultures is to have lived in that region, or in that country, for a substantial time. Reading about it on the Internet is not reassuring for your readers. You can bet that at least some of your readers have lived in the place you have transferred the action of your story, and will see right through your story. So instead of picking some remote jungle, try something closer to home, where you have lived and where you understand the ways of the inhabitants. Even to transfer the action to the other side of a country, as long as it is large enough, such as the United States, or Australia, or to another part of Europe, might achieve the same results for you without letting your readers down.

With the ease and relatively low cost of world travel these days, we can be in another country, in another part of the world, in less than twenty-four hours. And that's what makes writing fiction, particularly romance, so interesting. Why do we need to keep the main characters residing in a common area, having never moved from the region of their birth?

MATCHMAKING

Another thing that has changed rapidly over very recent years is the use of the Internet to find the 'perfect match'. Some such friendships and relationships work out very well. Others don't. There is no reason why two people who meet through an Internet contact need to live in the same region, although in real life this would of course be more practical. Many people are not concerned with being practical — they want results, and they want results that will satisfy their ideals of the perfect romance.

So if the girl is in the Philippines, or in China, or in Russia, there is no reason, indeed it is quite common, for a man in Australia, Europe or in the United States to make contact with her and meet her half way across the world. That's a challenge and is exciting in real life. It is just as exciting and as big a challenge in fiction.

RELATIONSHIPS

How can you determine what will work in a romantic story?

Think of what a relationship is. Or rather, think of what a good relationship should be.

A good relationship is not just two people living together in the same house, with their individual lives, their own lifestyles, coming together in the evening for dinner, and going out on their own. That's not a relationship. It is simply two people living in the same house, coming and going as they please. And that type of 'relationship' would be so boring, both in real life as well as fiction, that it wouldn't even be regarded as a romantic situation. You will want to introduce more elements of the romantic nature into your story. And that couple living together should think about introducing more elements into their true life situations.

A good relationship should be based on love, honesty, trust and commitment. Take away any one of those elements, and what you have left — the 'relationship' — falls apart.

There's your first possible angle for your fiction.

A good relationship is about sharing — people share the good times, the fun, the laughter. If they are not able to do that, then something begins to give at the seams.

A good relationship is all about doing things together. This is not to say that they should do everything together.

They are two people, but at the same time, they are individuals, with their own lives, their own friends, their own relatives, and their own work colleagues they will want to spend time with.

If one of the partners is so insecure that he or she insists they must do every single thing together, weaknesses will very soon begin to develop in their relationship.

Unfortunately these days in the real world, extramarital relationships provide more of the romance in one person's life than some partners, married or de facto, could ever provide.

A good relationship is taking the other person and helping them get more out of life, to introduce them to new experiences, new restaurants, new hobbies, new activities. Let them share many of these new experiences together. If they don't, and one doesn't want to share much with their partner, where is the romance? There probably isn't going to be much of a story here.

In the real world, not necessarily in novels, someone's idea of real romance is the period of months or years before a marriage and family are even contemplated. This period can be filled with different partners, lots of romantic conflicts. The very real need of choosing a partner out of several others could produce conflicts, for the other prospective partners who know or suspect they are about to be dumped, and the one who believes he or she might be the one the other will choose.

There are probably many more elements to a perfect relationship that I have not included here. Individuals will have their own set agenda of what makes for a good, secure relationship. Identify some of the weaknesses, and you have something you might be able to exploit in your story.

What is important to you in a relationship? Does your main character have that? If not, can you show how the absence of that ingredient might be affecting his or her welfare and happiness? Is it possible to make your main character want something desperately that you can identify as important?

POINT OF VIEW

Point of view is the part of the story from which you will relate the action. Who is the best person to tell the story? Is it from the point of view of one of the minor characters who knows both hero and heroine equally? Perhaps it is that omnipresent person who knows everything that is going on but is not really a part of the story? This will probably be the best point of view to use to narrate your story.

INTIMACY

Sex scenes are something that have evolved over recent years in romance stories. In the older stories, sex was not even thought of. Now, it is seldom that we could have a couple without some intimate contact. Think of your readers. How much detail, and how often, would they like to know all that the hero and heroine are getting up to? How much detail is enough? That depends. How much is too much? You might have to give sufficient thought to how much is just enough without alarming your readers, and without letting most of them down. Perhaps just subtle references to intimacy will be sufficient to get the message across. There is no magic formula for this part of the action. Intimate scenes should however be very important in the concept of the story you are telling.

CHECK YOUR STORY

Okay, you have just finished that story you have wanted to tell. Let's see if it would work for your readers and your publisher as well as it has worked for you.

Just as in all fiction, your story must be the high standard your readers expect. If you have written it well, have good strong characters, have enough conflict, a good plot, setting, and a satisfactory resolution, then you are way ahead of many other first-time writers.

Ask yourself a number of questions as you re-read your story after putting it in that top drawer for at least two or three months. Don't re-read it or edit it straight away. You will read it as a fresh story if you leave it for a few weeks.

Now, when you believe you have finished your story, give it a vital health check. Does the story work? Look at it. Consider every aspect of what you have written. Are you happy with it? Are you perfectly happy with it? Is there something you should have said differently? Is it too long? Is it too short? Are there scenes that don't really belong in the story? Have you written it well? Does it have meaning? Does the resolution meet the readers' high expectations? Is everything consistent with the characters, with the setting? What about the overall structure — are you happy with that too? Does it have purpose?

Did your story or novel hold your attention? If it did, you would probably have read it right through. If it didn't hold your attention, and you found yourself asking yourself why am I reading this, you can be sure that your readers would be asking themselves exactly the same question. If they wonder about your story on that point, they are most unlikely to read to the end. So go back and tidy up any areas that you thought were weak, or even missing.

Remember that as a new writer, you are unlikely to get the manuscript perfect in the first run. Many writers write, rewrite and then rewrite again and again until they are happy with the result. If you found some areas moving forward rather slowly, add some action. If the character seemed out of place, perhaps consider moving that section to a more appropriate place in the manuscript. If you found that everything happens in one chapter and there was nothing left for the rest of the novel, then spread it out and break down the story more. This now shows the benefit of proper planning even before you start to write. If you had had a proper plan, with the contents of each chapter set out, then the flow would most likely have been smooth, with the pace about even throughout.

WERE YOU A REAL STORYTELLER?

So, even though you have finished it, it is probably only the first draft, and will need a lot of work. But that's normal, so don't feel that you have failed as a writer. Most good writing comes from frequent rewrites. Be prepared to do your job and to finish off what you started.

When you reread your own story, consider what parts of it you enjoyed. And more importantly, think about those sections that you did not enjoy. This might not help you in this particular manuscript, but if you do consider your likes and dislikes, you can soon concentrate on these features in subsequent stories you tell. If characterisation was the part you liked most about this story, then you might prefer to concentrate on developing your characters in the next stories. Was it the way you wrote the dialogue? Then this might be one of the aspects of writing you could consider concentrating on in later stories.

When you list those sections of your story that you did not enjoy, see if you can overcome the problems and avoid them as much as possible in later novels.

How did you react to your manuscript when you re-read it after all those weeks? Did you enjoy the story? If not, it's not too late to change the story line. Did you think the characters were boring? Well, give them something interesting to do, and something interesting to say. If they are boring to you, and you were the one who created them, how do you think your readers are going to react? Probably the same way!

What was the best thing about the heroine? Was she bright and happy? Was she worthy of all the attention the hero of the story gave her? Was his response to her justified? If not, now is the time to reinvent the heroine.

And what about the hero? Did you like him? If you are a woman, then was he someone you would have liked to have gone out with and perhaps formed a relationship with? Was he the right hero for the heroine? Why? If you answer this question now, you will save yourself so much work in the next romance you write. So consider this first story as a trial run, with all (or at least most) of the blemishes removed from here on afterwards.

Would you really want to read another romance written by this same author (you)? If the answer is yes, then keep writing. If the answer was no, then rewrite your first draft and make it better, and stronger.

Probably the most important ingredient of a romantic story is you, the writer. How you wrote the story is what it is all about. Put ten writers together in a room and get them to write a story about something, and you will get ten different stories, with ten different outcomes, all written in totally different ways. Style is important, and so is your input in the way that you handle it. It will in many ways be your own personality coming through the story in a crafted way. Use your personality to feel empathy with the heroine. That way, readers will feel more warmth for her too. Think about your feelings as you get the characters to act, and your personality will come across. You really do become part of your own story without realising it. This will give your story warmth, and will result in a story that is full of emotion, and that's what your readers will be looking for—warmth, and emotion—either warmth and emotion that they will be able to relate to in their own lives, or crave because it is absent in their own lives. Make it personal, but make the story human. Tell it from the point of view of a real human being—yourself.

Chapter 6 The Detective Story

I f you want to play games with your readers, then write a detective story. It's a challenge, it's creative, and it's lots of fun. Regard your readers as your opponent.

The detective story is really an intellectual game you play with your readers, and one that you play on your own terms. The rules are simple. You can't deceive your readers, you can't make the outcome predictable, you must be fair, and you must respect the intellect of your opponent—your readers. Your readers will possess the ability to reason, otherwise they would not be reading your story.

Your opponent will try to keep one step ahead of you in your story, trying to guess the outcome, so you will have to give your readers the opportunity to prove that you are smarter than they are! It's a game for your readers, and it will be a game for you to try to outsmart him or her. That sounds like fun, doesn't it?

The rules to this game generally can't be broken except with a very good reason, and can only be broken if you offer your opponent something even more challenging.

Unlike those stupid, bumbling detectives of the third-rate television series of the 1960s and the 1970s and possibly later, the modern detective should be considered well educated and smart. After all, the detective has to outsmart his opponent — the criminal — and he or she must have incredible ability to reason, and will be quick to assess any situation. This is the twenty-first Century, and things have moved on quite a long way since the 1960s. So it's fair to say we can forget the image of those goofs.

Many crimes are solved by logical deductions, and by reasoning. If your detective lacks the ability to reason, then you won't get very far in your story. This is all part of the game you are playing — two equally well-matched people trying to outsmart one another, one (the criminal) trying to deceive the detective by covering his tracks, but bringing in deception to evade capture. You could never have your detective stumbling upon the culprit, without first applying all the reasoning that your readers would apply to bring the same culprit to justice. If your super-detective were to apply all his reasoning skills to solve the crime, and then he casually stumbles upon the villain, what are your readers going to think of the story? And more importantly, what are your readers going to think of you? You will have built up their hopes, and you will have wasted their time. They will not be very happy about that!

The modern criminal too (at least, those in your story) will be highly intelligent, manipulative, and will have the ability to outsmart even the most observant detective. In your story, the criminal will compete with the detective at every step of the story. And you will be the one who can make them determine their every move. You will be involved with the main characters from the moment the crime is committed, right up until the end when the criminal is brought to justice, or at least apprehended. Only you will know the outcome, but you wouldn't dare to even hint at whom the villain might be. Leave that up to your readers to see if they can guess the culprit. Your readers will also have to be convinced that the real culprit was brought to justice. Don't let your corrupt cop arrest the wrong person merely to clock up another arrest to make himself look good in the commissioner's eyes. You won't ever sell another book if your try that one on your readers!

Always, and I mean always, keep everything honest. Almost every day we read in the popular press that a victim was framed for a murder because of evidence that the investigating officer fabricated. He deliberately left evidence of his own at the scene of the crime merely to make a quick arrest to impress his supervising officers. I know that happens in real life — probably far more often than anyone would like to hear about, but you are not writing true stories — you are writing fiction that is going to be so clever it will impress your readers.

We often read about corrupt police officers, and those who frame criminals to escape their own arrest. Your story is not the place for corruption within the police force. Again, that could be the subject of your next novel, but certainly not this one. So rule out involving the detective in the crime. Detective stories don't work along those lines. To offset this, however, you could have a corrupt police officer being implicated in a crime, with another, completely honest detective, investigating him. That would be acceptable, but the investigating officer could not be the villain.

Your readers will have access to all the same clues that your detective has. You won't be able to tell your reader something, but withhold it from the detective. Your readers are, in many ways, equal to the detective, so must be given the same opportunities to solve the crime—even if the readers do try to beat the detective to the successful outcome of the case. So, no surprises, and no withholding evidence and clues.

Only the criminal is allowed to be deceptive, not you, Be honest with your readers at all times, but allow your criminal to get away with whatever he dares to try. The criminal can try to outsmart the detective, but you can't.

A crime story, or a detective story, is not a romance, or a travelogue, so love is not relevant to the story, or to the outcome, unless the criminal's partner is implicated in the crime in some way, either by being an accessory, or by trying to hide the criminal. But romance just for the sake of romance does not belong to this type of story. Leave that to your next novel.

You must kill off your victim in a known way. Don't invent a way of eliminating him that is not known, or should be fairly well known to the detective and to your readers. If your method of eliminating your victim is not believable, then your readers certainly won't believe it, and again your story will fail.

The cause of death can be creative, one that would require a little work to ascertain just how he met his fate. If you want a novel way of killing him off, and hold your readers in suspense at least until the end of the first chapter, you could make the detection of his death a little difficult, such as appearing that he electrocuted himself accidentally. It might not be until much later that one of the residents in his household tells the detective that he is a qualified electrical engineer and he should have known what he was doing. That can add tension to the story, and make the readers move on to at least the next chapter.

So, make sure you kill the victim off with a legitimate means. No fancy stuff here, no fantasy, no extreme fiction. Remember the readers have to at least try to guess how he died, and who killed him.

Your detective story must have a real investigator in it in the key role. The investigator could be a special agent of the FBI, or an agent from Interpol, but whatever you make him or her, he must be a real detective (at least in your readers' belief). He or she will have the ability to gather clues, to sift out the evidence, and make value judgements based on what has been found, and what is available. He could discard, momentarily, some of the clues that the readers will see as valuable, but might later go back and reassess those clues and begin to act on them. Remember as you write the story, your detective must gather clues, no matter how tiny they might be, sift through them, act on them, and come to some conclusion.

You shouldn't make those clues too obvious, they should be rather subtle, and appear at first to be of no value until they have been considered carefully, and weighed up for their contribution to solving the crime.

The storyline must be strong enough to carry the story for all its worth. So the crime must fit the value of the investigation. A trivial crime is not going to be worth the detective's time. So what's a good storyline for your detective story?

Murder is always a good standby. A body requires a lot of investigation, and your readers will know that this is the ultimate crime, and is truly worthy of solving, no matter how many weeks or months of investigation or how much the investigation will cost the taxpayer. Huge fraud could be okay, but quite often the main culprit is easy to detect with technology these days. Terrorism is common in the real world, but a story based on terrorism, real of imaginary, really belongs more in the realm of horror or thriller (depending on the outcome of the plot), but not detective story.

The difference between international spy rings and espionage, and your local killer, is that one is personal, the other is in the realm of international task forces and governments, involving much adverse publicity in the media, the source of endless television documentaries. You are writing a detective story, not an international best seller based on espionage.

So consider a body being found. After all, there will always be considerable investigative work required to find out the identity of the owner of the body, their last movements, their residence, their home life, family or friends, even before the detective begins looking for the culprit. And, of course, the post mortem (or autopsy) has to prove beyond doubt that the person was in fact murdered, and did not die from natural causes. Nothing would infuriate your readers more than if you spent two hundred pages telling your readers about the intricacies of the investigation, to have it revealed at the end of the story that there really was no crime to solve, the person simply stumbled over the embankment and died of a heart attack. That's rather weak, isn't it? So you will need a real crime (well, fictionalised of course), with a real victim (again fictionalised), with a full-scale investigation.

Use one detective, as more would get in the way of the story. Your readers will need to get inside the mind of your detective, to weigh up the same clues as your detective, so if more than one detective has the same evidence, but is looking at things from a different direction, your readers are going to get rather confused, and this will very soon detract from their enjoyment of the story. So employ one detective, but make sure that officer is a good one, with a good reputation of getting the desired results, and making your readers and the justice system very proud of him.

Solving the crime by logical deductions is the only outcome your readers will accept. Although people do seek the help of spiritual guides, the paranormal and so forth, these methods have no place in your story. Your readers will not be able to relate to the inner workings of your psychic, so don't employ one to do your work. Anyway, if your psychic did reveal the culprit on his first reading, then that would be the end of the story, with your readers left with nothing to solve. How disappointing would that be for them?

Remember, your readers must be able to match their own wits against those of the detective. A psychic's involvement, for example, would leave readers wondering why they ever bought your book. But if this first book you write is really good, you will want to write another one, and your readers will want to read it to get a good experience from the outcome. So write the story for your readers' enjoyment and intrigue.

The culprit should be known to the victim. His presence could be quite strong — he could have been an employee of the person, or even the employer. He could have been a family member who is always present and is always hanging around whenever the detective starts asking questions. By asking a lot of questions, the detective could give the culprit some clues about how he could further evade detection by outsmarting the detective without the latter even realising he is giving the culprit ideas in evading his next line of questioning. It is not fair to bring in the real culprit half way through the last chapter and expect your readers to have realised that it was him all along. Detective stories don't work like that. If your readers had never met the person before, how are they going to sum him up and assess his ability to have committed the crime? Make sure your readers are allowed to play the game — that's why they bought your book to read.

Through the years — is that through the decades? many detective writers have employed the butler or the gardener to commit the crime. These days, that person is not very original, and would not inspire the modern readers of detective stories. Bring in someone original, someone who will challenge the detective, and thus the readers, to really earn their week's wages in solving the crime.

Many themes have been murdered already. Themes such as family feuds have bored many a reader to death. The use of butlers and servants are stale and boring. Husbands and wives killing their partners have been killed off over their repeated use. In the early days of detective stories, wasn't it always the butler who did it? The butler's involvement these days is almost a joke if we can't find an answer to a simple outcome—where's it gone? Blame the butler—he did it. I can hear your readers yawning already as they close the book, never to open its covers again. Chauffeurs are not employed much these days, except by the very rich and famous, so it is less likely that the chauffeur would have much to do with killing off his employer. Think of something fresh, something that is not already dead through overuse, and something challenging.

Although the butler (or gardener) is too easy, and too obvious, the culprit should be someone of significance in the story. They should be an important person in the picture. They shouldn't be a minor, insignificant person who plays only a very minor part in the family feud or family problems. They should be active, but not obvious until that very last clue appears in the end of the book. And then your readers, at the same time as the detective, should be able to say to themselves, ah, yes, of course. Now wasn't he the obvious one? Why didn't I think of him before? The culprit could have been a prominent person in the local community, above reproach, and above suspicion. How could anyone have suspected such an honest person as him? The villain should, most importantly, be someone no one would reasonably suspect, perhaps because of their role in the community, that they are always seen as do-gooders, having an important role in helping the homeless, the elderly, and disadvantaged groups. Who would even suspect such an upstanding person in their community? They seem almost to hold up their community—how could anyone think like that of them? Yet in the real world, and in fiction, that's how life is. It's often those least suspected of committing a crime where you will find the real villain masquerading as a good and upstanding role model to which the rest of the community should aspire and model themselves on. Now, with such a villain, your story should be holding the readers' interest. And if this do-gooder were to help the detective in his investigation, and the detective never for once suspects him until that vital clue towards the end of the story, then your readers should be very happy with your story. After all, it is your readers you are writing it for, so if you can impress them with your creativity right at the end of the story, you will have done very well indeed.

No wonder I didn't think it could have been him! Well, now you know it was him, and you now realised that he fooled you as well as he fooled the detective.

The culprit could never be someone who is just as obvious to the detective or the readers. It couldn't be someone with a criminal background to such an extent the readers could logically imply that the latest crime was only one small step removed from all his other previous misdemeanours. You couldn't employ a psychopath to commit a grisly murder—he would be just too obvious. And you couldn't use a mentally retarded person to do the work of a killer—it would be hard to interrogate him, and the result would be too obvious to your detective as well as to your readers.

Although you will have only one detective, how many culprits can you use? If you have a series of similar crimes, you should stick to one villain. If the crimes are dissimilar, then your readers might not guess that they could have been committed by the same person. One type of crime, one villain is the best formula. The villain though might not have been working alone. He could have had accomplices who did not overtake the major role from him, but nevertheless had some input into the crime being investigated.

Be fair to your readers. You can't have the villain hiding behind some masquerade that we knew nothing about in the early part of the novel. You can't have him hiding as a Mafia agent with the other thugs protecting him at all costs. A story like this simply won't work, your readers won't appreciate it, and they certainly won't appreciate you as a writer. So no secret societies, no escaping overseas and working for a foreign agency. This is the realm of spying, and is a totally different genre from what you are trying to write. Don't move your villain overseas because it is so easy for the investigating officer to lose track of him and your story will fail. The villain has to be hanging around and be present at all times, or at least his presence in the general vicinity should be assumed. If you move him right away from the action, you have effectively killed off the story and that will be the end of it, and possibly the end of you as a writer.

The investigating police detective must always be looking out for clues. So should your readers. If you don't give both at least an adequate number of clues to go on, then what is the point of the book? Probably none, because if your readers believe that he will never find the cause of death or the culprit, then he probably won't even look for them. It is surprisingly easy to close a book and put it back on the bookshelf without finishing it.

Depending on how you handle the situation, it should

be fairly legitimate to give false clues that the detective follows, only to find that he has wasted a lot of time pursuing the wrong lead. It happens in real life, so there is no reason why it can't happen in your story.

How much extraordinary detail do you need to include in a mystery story? Imagine yourself in the place of the detective. Imagine what he would be following, and what he would be looking at. He would not be taking side trips to the other side of the world to meet his prospective new partner, nor would be be taking off from Auckland to New York for the weekend to see his children. That might happen in real life, but he would most certainly have a reason for his escape, and it would have to be sanctioned by his hierarchy. So if his trip from New Zealand to New York for three weeks holiday is not part of the investigation, then it is certainly not a part of your story.

During the story your readers will want to know about the detective, so you should weave points about him throughout the story. Is he one for sticking to the case no matter what gets in his way? Is he one who gives up easily and takes the easy option, only to find his villain anyway? Has he had numerous successes with previous investigations? Does he have a tendency to solve every case he investigates? Your readers will want to know what type of person he is dealing with on both sides of the crime.

And your potential villains. Describe all likely villains, but not in three or four straight paragraphs. Weave their likes and dislikes, their strengths and weaknesses, and their true personalities into the story, but do so subtly. Don't give your readers, or the detective, any biases. Don't make it so obvious they should both assume the villain to be one person because you have overemphasised him in the story. Don't give your readers even a hint at who it could possibly have been, because if you do, your detective would have come to the same conclusion and arrested him in chapter one ... and end of story. Sorry, readers, there is no more. Sorry about that! Deduction must be the only way the readers and the detective can both come to the same conclusion — at the right time, which just happens to be at the end of the story.

However, with your descriptions of characters, and the victim, you must make them legitimate people. That is, they must sound like real people, however you define that. Remember that if you put one hundred people in a room, every one of those people will be different. They will have different agendas in similar circumstances. They will have quite different personalities. They will have different motives for everything they do. And each one of them could have been the culprit. They could all have been likely candidates, and that's what your readers will be looking for.

Don't give one of the potential suspects a long criminal history, expanding on his history at every chance you get to mention him, only to let him off the hook in the end. You are persuading your readers that they should invest their efforts into catching him, and then you would let them down. How dare you!

If you could say after you re-read your own manuscript that it all sounds feasible, that you haven't created anything too stupid, too far fetched, too improbable, or so stale, and the story is original, then you could have created a story that is worth reading. But how many times do we see the same evidence, and the same clues, used over and over for third-rate television series? It's rather boring after the twentieth time, if not before.

You must come up with something fairly original, and then embellish it so that as a whole, it becomes original. It isn't at all difficult if you give this point some thought. Think of something you don't hear about too often, and give it a twist.

A source of criminal tendencies could be police journals that should be located in your main city library, or at least in the national library of your own country. By law, legal deposit demands that one or two copies (sometimes more) of every publication published in a country should be deposited with the library within a specified time, such as within two months of publication. So if you are near the National Library of Australia in Canberra, the National Library of New Zealand, or the Library of Congress in Washington, or in any other capital city and possibly a state library in many countries, do a thorough search of the library's holdings to locate the police journals. And then go through a few piles of them to find out about the extraordinary cases and interesting investigations officers have carried out, criminal profiles and so on. Yes, you will be delving into the dark and sinister and low side of city life, but that's what life is like, so you have no excuse not to make your story dark and sinister and based on low life. But that's what you embarked upon when you decided to write your detective story!

Chapter 7 The Short Story

One of the things about writing the short story that many writers enjoy is that they can be rather creative, without having to go into endless details, with convoluted plots, character development and long pieces of dialogue. The short story seems to fill that gap for them where they can be creative in a pleasant way and really excel in the process.

The short story has a little in common with the novel, but also a lot that is not similar to the novel. Both, despite the fact that they are both works of fiction, that is, works straight from the creative person's imagination, are different. Both provide stimulation to the writer, both forms of literature provide stimulation to the reader. Both forms of writing are equally acceptable.

BE CREATIVE WITH YOUR STORY
The reason writers create the short story is simply that they want to develop their creativity, and they want to tell a story — that story that really must be told. This should be the criteria for any form of fiction.

Sometimes a short story can be very long. At the same time, some writers create short novels. And often in between these two, both overlap.

The novel has its challenges that a short story doesn't. Being a shortened form, a short story can only be an excerpt from a life, not a life itself. A short story cannot span two or three generations. It cannot span two decades.

A typical short story can show that excerpt from a life, and related incidents in that life, that encompasses all relevant goings on over a period of a day, sometimes even less, or perhaps a few days. It is a story about one incident, few characters, at one time.

Because short stories are, almost by definition, short, they must not so long they actually become short novels. In a novel, the writer has time to develop the characters. In the short story, no such luxury is permissible because of the lack of space, or length. Setting must be fixed — the characters cannot go travelling around the world to meet their beloved in another country. The short story takes place usually in one location, although hints can be brought into the writing to suggest that one or more characters have just come back from a more distant location.

If you are writing short stories, and hope to get them published in popular magazines, you will be writing the story not for the reader initially, although that will be your end goal, you will be writing the story for the editor of the magazine you want to have it published in. If you write for the editor, and can get past the editor, then your story may be published.

So read a few stories the editor has published, and ascertain what types of stories they are, how they are structured, and the general theme of them. And then try to match them, but with your own creativity. Readers read fiction to be entertained. If you can entertain the readers, but first of all entertain the editor, then you may stand a better chance of winning.

So read lots of magazines or anthologies that you would like to write for, and look at the stories included. Don't just read the stories you like. It's a bit like watching bad television. It is often easier to work out what we don't like about a third-rate television program that grates on our nerves, than it is to decide what it is that we do like about a half-hour's supposed entertainment.

Not everyone will like every story, and not everyone will like every television program.

A novel is seldom read in one sitting (unless the reader is a fast, speed reader, has lots of time, or is sick and is in bed for a few days). A short story, by contrast is taken in at one reading.

Because the writer is writing more or less to a length, the story must contain not one word that does not belong in it. Every word must say what the writer intended, and must mean something. There is no room in a short story for irrelevancies, side-tracking, and incidents that don't contribute directly to the actual story being told.

In the short story, because of the limitations of space and number of words, even the first sentence must get right into the story. The first paragraph must tell the readers significant information about what they might expect as they read on. And most importantly, the first paragraph must grab the readers' attention so strongly that it won't let them go. It must make them want to read on, and read right through to the end.

BEFORE YOU BEGIN

That first paragraph must set the scene, introduce the main character, and possibly the theme and the tone of the rest of the story.

The end of the short story should be just that. When the climax is reached, when the conflict is resolved, when things come to a head, then that's it — the end of the short story. Sorry, there is no more. There is no place for wrapping up, bringing warring factions back together and allowing the readers to see how they are getting on in their lives several months after the story has ended. The ending is really that — the story ends.

A short story will have the minimum number of characters. Here, the writer might introduce one main character, one or two minor characters, but seldom more. The writer can, however, imply that thousands of people are present, but they are not really characters — more a background noise. Take, for instance, a scene at a union rally. We know there would be hundreds of union members there, the writer can imply the size of the crowd, with their jeering and booing at management, but that's not the same as having hundreds of characters in the story. And most importantly, each and every character a writer brings into the short story they are creating, must do something, or their presence must have a purpose. In the short story, it is acceptable to have a character whose presence is imminent, but who is instilling fear and pain on the others in the story in their anticipation. Although in such an example the person is not present as a character, his or her pending presence works the same as a real character to create tension and anticipation.

In the short story, it is a pity if the reader becomes very interested in a character, and by the end of the story that particular character has contributed little or nothing to the story. That character's role could be better served in the readers' mind and their imaginations if that particular character could be combined with one of the other characters who did belong in the story, and who had a real part to play in it.

The short story must be self contained. The writer could refer to some incident before the story takes place, but that's not the same as saying that long scenes before the main part of the story begins are acceptable. They are not. No, a good short story will be self contained — no story before it, nothing to follow on from it. It really is an excerpt from a much longer part of life.

A writer of good short stories will have special talents. The main talent here is the ability to ensure that not one word is included in the story that does not belong there. Not one sentence of dialogue should be included if it does not have a major role to play in the story and to move it along. And not one description can be included unless it has a significant impact on the story. In other words, the shorter it is to tell the same story, the better. This aspect of the short story is what makes a short story great — great for the writer to create it, and great for the readers to read it.

Readers will have expectations. Those expectations must be met by the writer. If they are not, then the writer has let down the readers. And wouldn't that be a disappointment?

YOU NEED ACTION!

Action, if there is any action, cannot be drawn out beyond its usefulness.

If there is any action ... Action can be anything. It can be different things to different people. It will be interesting, but without a lot of moving parts. It could be sedentary, a dialogue perhaps, a job interview. It could be two people relating to one another with different views.

Don't expect to write the perfect, gripping short story on your first sitting. It probably won't happen unless you are a born story teller. And if you were the perfect born story teller, you would probably have written numerous short stories already. You will need a lot of patience to write a good short story. You will develop the craft over a long period, and quite likely, after numerous attempts to write short stories.

Writing the short story would be the ultimate test of a writer's creative skills. Some people come into short story writing on the assumption that they will just sit down for half an hour, type out a few hundred words, and there's their short story. How disappointed those writers will be. How disappointed their readers will be.

A short story can be one of suspense, investigation, delving into the unknown. Some of the writers from the past were masters at the suspense short story — Edgar Alan Poe for example created some brilliant short stories that were far from sedentary pieces of writing. They were full of suspense, full of action that was appropriate to the story, with characters who blended in with the action, the setting and the theme of the story. But to begin with, unless you have that ability to write a short story with such qualities, take it easy until you have mastered the art of story telling.

Early in the short story, create a scene in which the character develops, a setting in which to place the main character, and the situation (that is, the plot), in which the main character has to work and do his job of satisfying the readers. That's a lot to put in to the opening, but it can be done with the careful craftsmanship of writing and rewriting and simplifying your prose.

The opening should lead gracefully (at least in literary terms) into the second paragraph and the next stage of the story. This will be where you develop that first scene and add new but crucial elements to your story. Remember, you don't have many words to play with here, so get right into it.

THE FIRST PARAGRAPH

Early in the story — usually within the first paragraph, or paragraph two at the most, the readers would most likely want to know what's likely to happen. They will need to receive some clues about where the story is likely to lead so they can remain interested and will want to read right to the end of the story.

Although the readers will want to know what's likely to happen, this is not the same as telling them what will definitely happen. That part of the story should be allowed to evolve throughout the rest of the story. After all, if you tell the readers what will happen, then they will quite rightly ask what was the point of reading the story, and why did you even bother to write it? Keep some of the mystery aside for them to develop their own images of the scenes and action you create. Let them picture likely outcomes, and let them think about what they are reading. Allow them to use their vivid imaginations — your readers will be bright people, who are alert, and will need to work on the story they are reading.

THE READER CREATES THE SCENES
Because a short story is just that, be very economical with your words. This is where creative writing can be at its best. You have to economise with expressions, with words, with characters. So, for example, instead of long descriptions of scenes, you can cut out a lot of words by making descriptions part of the whole — in other words, show, don't tell. Instead of giving a description of the long coastline, describe the main character expecting to take four hours to walk along the coast and climb down that last headland he can just see through the sea mist in the distance. This short description tells us that the character is on foot, that the coastline is long, it is many kilometres from where the person is to where he or she wants to go, and we know that the cliffs are reasonably high because he has to scale down that last one. A few words, lots of description. By writing in this way, you not only develop your own creativity, but you make the readers do a lot of the work. Get the readers to create the scenes from the brief descriptions you give for their guidance. On the other hand, the descriptions have to be complete enough for the readers to form at least a vivid picture in their minds. It is

pointless giving so few details that the reader is unable to imagine the setting, or even what might be happening.

DEVELOPING YOUR CHARACTERS

Look around you, wherever you might be. You might be in a supermarket queue waiting to reach the checkout. Is there a short story there? You bet there is! That person in front of you — what is their life about? How are they going to get through that hurdle this evening when they have to face an important decision with their partner? Or that shopper who is just leaving the supermarket. She is lame. She has an important issue in her life that is just about to come to a head this very afternoon. Be creative. This is creative writing at its best, so make the most of it. Be creative, and invent stories to go around the people you meet, in the places you frequent.

Buy yourself a cup of coffee and enjoy that — but make sure you take your notebook with you, because you will be coming up with numerous stories, many characters, and a whole lot of action for your stories.

Look at that woman drinking her coffee right in front of you. She looks sad. What caused her sorrow? There's a story. Or the woman with the two children. The children don't belong to this planet, because they are perfectly behaved and polite. What is her story? Perhaps her lover has just proposed to her, and she has to make that decision — and how will the children fit in? And there too is another short story.

Ride your bicycle to the shop. You'll probably meet another cyclist on his or her way. That other person might be having trouble riding up the hill. What is her story?

Imagine that everyone has a story to tell, and that everyone is so eager to tell you their story. You will be able to get something out of each and every one of these individuals. So make the most of every person, every incident, every setting you come across, and from every story they could tell you if you listened to them. Make sure you always add the 'little things' too, because these are the ingredients that will bring your story to life, and make it seem as if your story really is about real people. And if anything you come across in your everyday life shows promise, jot it down in your notebook. After all, that's why you carry it with you.

Let's now look at the main ingredients of the short story. We have considered the criteria for such a story — brevity, one incident, minimal number of characters, simple setting, and the importance of letting the readers do a lot of the work by creating the images for themselves.

The plot is what happens in your story. What is the main action? Remember, in a short story, it doesn't have to be a complex plot — a simple story will work well. Plot too is often worked around the theme of the short story. Although these two ingredients are separate, they are tied in together. The theme will determine whether the story will be a suspense story, one with a romantic element, or simply, an excerpt from the life of someone.

TAKE EXCERPTS FROM LIFE

Many years ago, Richard Burton narrated the story in the film *Ode To Two Minutes*. It looked at a two-minute excerpt from a whole range of different people's lives at one particular time, on one particular day. So in your own two-minute ode, you could include excerpts from a range of different people doing all sorts of different things. Someone getting ready to go to work. A bride getting ready for her wedding. Perhaps another one was attending a funeral. How good is your imagination? Perhaps you could make your *Ode To Two Days*.

Back to the plot. The plot is what happens in the story. It's where everything happens, and it determines what happens, and why it happens. All the scenes and the actions of the story lead comfortably into the theme.

A story, with a good plot, and the theme you have chosen, has to be set somewhere. The setting—where the story is located at the time of the story—must be true to the plot, or to the story you are telling. It must be an integral part of the whole. Take away the setting, and often the plot fails. If the setting is not right for the plot, the whole story could collapse. So the setting must reflect the plot.

You need a character, or at least one main character. The plot, the theme, will make the character act the way they do, and behave with certain characteristics. These characteristics could be the norm for that person, but remember that the character will react to the environment he or she encounters. The person might find himself pushed well out of his comfort zone, where he could not be expected to react appropriately. He might even say things under these circumstances that one would not expect him to blurt out. Don't we all do that under the right conditions?

As your story develops, readers will want to know more about that character. Who is that person you have created? Why did you create him or her? What is so special about that one person? Why couldn't you have selected someone else for that main role the person is playing? Your readers will want to know all these things about that character. How did he get into the story?

DIALOGUE

All characters say something. At least, most people do, and some say plenty. In our everyday lives, many people love to chatter on about ... well, nothing really special. We all know people like that. But in a short story, there is no room for idle chatter. And if you include dialogue that doesn't contribute to the story, your readers will get bored with the story, and rather angry with you. You need to keep your readers happy — you might need them for the next story you write!

Dialogue in fiction, the short story as well as a novel, is important in several ways. It imparts information to the readers. It tells the readers attitudes, and location. It tells readers about the mood of the character. It can be — should be — used effectively to move the story forward without long pieces of narrative.

Good dialogue in fiction is not one person just saying something for the sake of it. Good dialogue is one person reacting to what another said. A character speaks, the other character reacts to what is said. And then the first character responds — or reacts to what that one said. Do that in your story until a picture is built up, word by word. Make the dialogue interesting. Make it convey everything you can make it — mood, feelings, setting.

If you have more than one character in your short story, you should consider using dialogue for all the benefits that good dialogue imparts to a story. Otherwise those two or three characters are just there, not really part of the story, just sitting it out until pay-day, or any other way they want to fill in the time. If they are part of the one scene, they will interact, and good dialogue is all about interacting with other characters.

POINT OF VIEW

Who is going to tell your story? Who is the best person to tell it? If it is very personal, you could have the main character tell the story. That way, you could bring out inner feelings and emotions to everything that is happening, or is about to happen. Often a first-person point of view works well for a short story, whereas it might not work well in a longer work of fiction such as a novel.

If you have several characters, perhaps two or three, and each is contributing to the story, you could consider the third-person point of view, often called the third-person omniscient—which just means the third person, or the story teller, is hidden. You don't see that person, they are not part of the action or the story, that are just someone who is employed for the duration to tell the story.

But before you even begin to write your short story, you must decide on the point of view. If you find that one particular point of view does not work, tell the story through the eyes of another person. You could use another one of the characters, perhaps a minor character, to describe the action, and through that person, describe how the other characters feel through the way they act. That story-teller could be sitting just on the edge of the story, watching the world around them go by. Tell the story through someone like that.

If at first your story does not work because you have used the wrong point of view, you will probably find that if you change this one aspect of your story, the result will be so much better.

CHARACTERS

Characters are what the short story is all about. Without characters, there is no point in writing a story. A setting on its own won't stimulate any reader's imagination. So what does your character do on a person level? Does he slur his speech? Is he hard to comprehend, thus a possible theme for the story? Is he always telling jokes that everyone has heard many times before? Does he wear his scarf around the wrong way? Does he always forget to comb his hair before he goes out anywhere? Descriptions such as these are what make that person human. And we are all individuals, so make your characters all individuals. There are some people who would like everyone else to be just like them—they cannot tolerate the thought of anyone being different, being an individual. That's okay in a story—this could be what is creating the level of conflict with those who want to be slightly different.

We all show things like strengths and weaknesses in different ways. Is your character weak? How is he weak? Is he timid? How? Show through examples how your character is timid, holding back from doing anything expected of him through fear of being put down and ostracised by the threatening tones of others around them. Again, these are things that make us individuals, and make us all human. If we were all identical—clones of that one person who would prefer to see us all alike, thinking alike and doing everything the same, wouldn't our story be boring? Yes, very boring indeed!

A GUIDE TO STORY TELLING

Editors and publishers will buy a story or manuscript for these reasons:

The story will give the readers what they expect. Remember what we said about pleasing the editor first, the readers second? So make sure you please the editor of the magazine you want to write for.

The story has a character (usually a likeable person) with whom the readers can identify. If the readers like the main character, and can identify with that person, they are more likely to enjoy the story. They will feel comfortable reading what they like, about characters they like.

The main characters solve their problems by their own efforts. We admire this quality in real people — those who are not always dependent on others to hold their hand in every crisis they face. Your readers will like this type of character more if they can see real humanness in the person.

The story makes the readers glad they read it, therefore giving them what they wanted from that magazine.

Your short story could be rejected for one of many reasons. Consider these reasons. They are all used at some time or other in the story-buying process magazines go through. The same reasons are given by book publishers.

You probably sent the editor an unsolicited story. It is always advisable to send a query letter to the editor of a magazine first, to see if he or she really wants yet another story. Often magazine editors are swamped with stories from all over the country, and sometimes from all over world. They already have plenty to chose from. So ask if they want another one to consider. Tell them briefly about your story in no more than one page, but tell them why yours is going to be so much better that any they have already received. Here, concentrate more on the story, not about yourself generally, unless you are an up and coming story teller that most editors have already heard about. In that case, you could get away with concentrating on yourself more than on the story you are offering.

You probably didn't send the story through a literary agent. Unfortunately, these days editors and publishers save time and cut costs by getting others to do the work they used to do as part of their job. Now, they see the role of literary agent as the story sifter for them, sending them only those stories that are really great and that don't need much work. This way they receive only very few, compared with hundreds or perhaps thousands of stories over a year. I am sure you can see their point, but as a new writer, that's just one more obstacle in your path to success. And because you might not be well known in the publishing world, many literary agents do not take on previously unpublished writers, no matter how good they might be. After all … no one has ever heard of them, so the editors, and publishers, and the readers of magazines and books haven't either. So how do you get your story accepted?

It's not well written. Fair enough, you couldn't expect an editor to buy something that was sloppily put together, could you? The story you write must be the very best that anyone could possibly write. It must be free of all mistakes, free of ambiguities, and all those blemishes I have pointed out.

The story does not meet the publisher's requirements. It is essential to look at the magazine's requirements to see just what they are publishing before wasting postage sending off your story to the wrong publication. Good writing does not compensate for bad choice of magazine. Don't send a romance story to an editor who wants Western stories, unless it has a romantic Western theme.

Editors reject stories, no matter how well written they might be, because they feel that the particular story will not give their readers what they want or expect from that particular magazine. Editors know their magazines, and they know their readers. Many readers give them feedback, so over only a few issues, editors get a feel for what their readers want, and are looking for. How dare they give their readers anything else instead?

The editor is merely the go-between the writer and the readers. He or she might act as a referee on the readers' behalf, and select stories they believe their readers will want to read. This is similar to the point above.

The pace of the story was wrong. You might have tried to cram too much into the few pages available for a short story, or you really tried to write a condensed novel in six pages. Or it was too long for what you actually said. You must always check the pace and keep it consistent. It should be consistent with the theme, and the type of story, and the setting. Don't have a racy story set in a boring office, or a fast pace set at a yoga class. And don't have a story with a slow pace where the main character is fighting for his or her life. Your own feel for the story will help dictate the true pace you should aim for when telling your story.

The story was not complete in itself. You left your readers up in the air as to what happened. Readers want to know if your main character was saved, lived to tell another story, or did something that was in keeping with his or her personality. Always make sure your conclusion is valid, and clear. But occasionally, you might write a story where the whole mystery of what happens is left up in the air for the readers to speculate. Sometimes, if this ending is justified, it can be effective. But make sure that it really is the ending you were hoping to achieve.

You may have had character problems. This comes down to not really knowing all your characters. It might be that you don't know how they will act in the circumstances you put them into, or how they would react when confronted with one of the other characters, or with the weather. In real life, we all adapt, but some do so better than others. If your character didn't adapt to their situation, then that might be a reason for a problem with a character.

Your main character might not have been real enough, or identifiable. If you are creating exceptional characters, then you have to work even harder for your readers to think of them in the same way that you did when you created them.

Perhaps you had too many characters for a short story. Remember that if you have too many characters doing too much, readers soon lose track of who is doing what to whom. There is no real formula to say how many characters you should have for a certain number of pages. Use your discretion here, or your general feeling about how many people are just right. You can, of course, 'pool' a lot of characters, such as those in an office could speak with one voice, that voice telling the readers the thought, or thoughts, of the whole pool of characters. A school class, too, could act as 'the class', as a single character, rather than thirty or so children.

The number of characters should be proportional to the length of the story. The longer the story, the more characters you are able to introduce safely. But please don't overdo the number of characters just because you like them. Put some of them into your next story! If your characters are really great, especially those you created for the occasion, but they don't really fit into a particular piece of writing, don't despair and think you have wasted your time. You probably haven't. A good writer can take any character, adapt them to another situation, and there they are in a new life. You might find that if your characters don't fit one story, you can create another story around them.

The editor could not get interested enough in the characters to care what happened to them. Yes, there are stories like that, and television programs like that. They seem to be very ordinary people, leading very ordinary lives, in a very ordinary setting, doing very little. Write the story again with vigour next time!

Nothing much happened in the story. You simply wrote a narrative about ... well, nothing in particular, really. Unfortunately, even a well-written piece of fiction does not stand on its own. It has to convey something to the readers, something that makes the readers say, 'wow! I am glad I took the time to read that.'

The characters did not have anything much to resolve, or did not resolve it by their own means. But a story about a person who has everything resolved for him could show him to be a rather weak, useless type, or one who has so much power in his circle that he commands such respect that all these things are done for him. Both these characters are viable in a well-written story that is set around them. The conflict comes about from their attitude, or their lack of attitude about anything, their lack of emotion. This, of course, comes down to how well you have developed your character, and your story. Both must be consistent with one another. They both must enhance one another, with plot and character working well together and enhancing what one offers to the other, whether the character enhances the plot, or vice versa.

The story was just too depressing, too gruesome, littered with tragedy, blood and gore and corpses. Sometimes such stories do find a market, but check your market for such a story before you begin to write one with this type of theme. However, with changing social attitudes, and different generations of readers demanding differing things from their entertainment, this type of story could find a ready market in the very near future.

The story was offensive. In other words, it was in very poor taste. You obviously haven't taken any notice of the style that a particular magazine wanted. Nor have you considered your potential readers. Give the readers, and the editor, or publisher, exactly what they want.

The plot of your story is weak. This is a very common mistake, especially with writers early in their careers. The story might seem fine to the writer, but it is often wise to ask someone else who is completely honest with you, just what they think. But make sure you ask the right person to assess it. There are many, many people out there who would like to put someone else down because they are doing something they themselves would like to do, but can't. So make sure your assessor is well-suited and honest.

You have told it in a way that is unclear, confusing or offensive. Although you know what you are trying to say, doesn't mean that anyone else will get the same meaning, and make sense of what you have written. Remember that you are only one person in the long chain of things that will lead to potential publication. Although the story might work for you, this is no guarantee that it will be received with the same enthusiasm by anyone else, least of all the editor or publisher. But then again, we all have different standards. And just because one person says it is terrible, this does not always mean that it really is all that bad. But it could be! It could be worse than the editor has told you, and he or she is merely being polite. So please assess the comments critically, and get someone else to criticise your writing also, to see if they too agree with the editor. Remember that editors are human, and suffer from the same faults and shortcomings as we all do.

The editor couldn't read your story because it was typed with … and you forgot to put your name on it and … and … Please look at the check list included in this book! See if anything on that list is missing in your story.

Your opening paragraph was too slow and the editor fell asleep before turning the page. This is a common fault. Fiction does not enjoy the luxury of slow starts. If it does, then it will have to be a very desperate editor who will publish a story that is so slow and painful in the beginning. After all, he will ask, when does the real story start? Perhaps it doesn't.

The story simply grated on the editor's nerves and she hated it! Ask yourself why you sometimes turn off a movie that has been praised to the heavens, or throw down a short story or a book that has come from the pen (or more correctly these days, from the computer) of a famous story-teller. It's the same thing. A story that appeals to one person might have the opposite effect on the editor. Consider the editor's comments carefully before taking them to heart and brooding over the fact that the editor has told you, in effect, that you can't write. We all have bad days, and will be in a bad mood for any number of reasons. Perhaps this was the editor's off day. You can never tell what the other person was thinking, and you might, after all, have written something really great.

Or simply, there just wasn't really a good reason why it was rejected. Sorry about that. We really are! Yes, I know, no reason might be a valid reason. We can't think of why we don't like it, but believe me, we don't like it. The reason could be hard to define. If this is the reaction from an editor, try revising the manuscript, or, better still, rewriting it from the very first word and see if the next draft is better. You could be surprised.

The main character is not likeable enough. Your reader wants to be able to identity with the way in which your main character solves his or her problem. A nasty type will get his just treatment in the end, but it doesn't always happen in real life. But it could. If your readers could see that justice is done to your villain, they might begin to like that person. A really nice person can go through hell and back again, but as long as all goes well for that character in the end, the readers will be happy, because the resolution was what they wanted. A final twist, a new direction for the character might be all that's needed to save the story.

The odds are not insurmountable enough, or the editor does not believe they are sufficiently insurmountable. Don't fake the problem! Make it believable, make it real, even though the story is fiction. Yes, I realise that sounds like a bit of contradiction, but the character has to seem real, and the trials of life for the main character must seem real.

The main character does not solve her problems by her own efforts. They are solved for her by one of the minor characters. Weak! This deprives the readers of the pleasure of feeling for the main character, admiring her after all she has gone through, just to find someone beat her to the resolution. We all look up to someone who can solve their own problems in life and come through as a different, and stronger, person. In fiction, this applies equally well. So take out the character, or characters, who are always doing things for others, and make the person stand on their own two feet. But of course you could have a story about someone who is kind to others, and their friends like to pamper them, but you have to decide in your own story how far you can take this kindness. Take it too far, and the story disappears. Funny, that!

The resolution is predictable, leaving nothing for the reader to get excited about. If the story is that predictable, why did you bother to write it? This is fiction, so the fiction can make you stretch the truth, and make you create a real story. So go ahead and create that story.

The goal is weak—there has to be real conflict that needs to be resolved. If it is too weak, the story just won't work. In fact, you probably won't even have a story! Again, you should ask yourself why you even bothered to write the story. Write it with a real story in mind. Make it exciting. Make it anything other than a boring, real-life soapy standard. Make it a really good story to tell.

And as a checklist for your own guidance, consider this list. For all the stories you write, ask yourself these questions:

- Is the title effective, appropriate and catchy?
- Does the story work?
- Is it long enough to handle all the action and conflicts?
- Is it too long?
- Are there any unnecessary words?
- Are there any clichés ?
- Would it appeal to the intended readers?
- Would the story hold readers' attention until the end?
- Would readers think about the story after they have read it?
- Would readers be able to relate to the story?
- Would readers be able to relate to the characters?
- Is there anything in it that is unnecessary — anything that does not carry the story along?
- Is the punctuation about right?
- Are the lengths of sentences about right?
- Are the lengths of paragraphs varied, and about right?

- Are the words too complicated?
- Does it have a smooth flow ... introduction, middle and conclusion?

Apply this questionnaire to your story when you have finished it!

Use this questionnaire for each of your stories. It will help keep you on the right track!

PUTTING TOGETHER YOUR STORY

Now, let's get down to the most enjoyable part — writing your short story, using all the guidelines you have learned up to this point.

This is the fun bit. It's where you bring your characters and their dialogue into the setting you created, and add the conflict we talked about earlier. These components of your story now all come together.

And it is here you will appreciate the value of giving so much attention to developing those special people, and that unique setting in your story.

Your story can be any length, but it should be long enough for the conflict to be resolved in an acceptable way. Well, acceptable to your readers at least. It may not necessarily have to be resolved to the same extent we would like it to be fixed up in our own private lives.

Your story should be long enough for the characters to be able to fully develop, there should be no loose ends at the time, leaving your readers asking themselves ... 'well, so what ... what was that all about?'

So far we have looked at all the ingredients of creative writing — theme, point of view, the characters, their dialogue — who says what and how and to whom, where the story is set and so on.

But good writing is never a block of each of these components standing alone.

Your job as a creative writer writing your story is to tie each of those aspects together in the cleverest way possible, to weave the theme through the characters, to bring the characters together with the setting, and show how they act, and why, and how they grate on each others nerves. It is your job to show your readers that you have created a story they will really want to read. It is in your creativity that they will turn to time after time to get the entertainment they want in their reading. This might even be your very first story or novel. If it's really good, and let's hope it will be, then they will look for your name on stories and books in the future. Now isn't that something worthwhile to aim for with your writing? It sure is!

You have written your short story. Congratulations. Well done! What are you going to do with it?

You can try looking for a market for it in some literary magazine. You could expect to earn a few dollars from the process if you can get it published.

While you send your short story off to a magazine and wait for the editor to decide whether yours is the story of the month, write your next one.

When you have finished that one, write the next one.

Magazines that do publish short stories usually have lots of them to choose from. There are usually lots more short stories out there than there are publishing opportunities.

Don't be discouraged. If you want to write short stories, then write short stories. Lots of them.

When you have written enough of them, consider self-publishing them in a book. See Chapter 16 on self-publishing to give you an incentive to keep writing. And see Chapter 15 on marketing to see how you could make it all work out for yourself. To see your first short story in print is one thing, but to see a whole selection of your short stories in a book that you have published is a reward you should strive for.

Just because your story is not published by a magazine should not deter you from developing your creativity. I once told a writing friend that she should not be held back by what's not going to happen. Unless you are extremely lucky, and extremely well known to readers and to editors, you are going to find it difficult to get a market for your short stories in the commercial world.

Make sure your short stories are worth publishing, and are worth reading. Readers are going to invest several hours of their time reading your stories, so you have to give them something that they are going to enjoy, and will take a great delight in reading.

If you please your readers with originality, you will have succeeded. If you don't, then you will have failed.

Chapter 8 Children's Books

Writing children's literature can be rather challenging. Authors who do so will be rewarded with books that give pleasure to many, many children. It's not only the children themselves who enjoy the stories. Parents and the grandparents enjoy reading to children, and enjoy the stories too, probably as much.

Writing for children is different from writing normal fiction, because young people's minds are usually so active, and they are full of emotion.

Children's stories are an ideal way of influencing young minds in a positive way. Give them something to look forward to in their lives, show them that there really is a lot of good out there in the real world, and you will make a vast difference to those minds.

There can be positive messages, no matter what age you want to write for. They enjoy positive stories about family life. You might like to, through your story, show how an animal helped a small child recover from a dreadful and serious injury or illness. It might be the story of how a family pet always protected the family, and particularly the child when he or she was threatened with danger from outside the family home. But don't make the story too threatening, or too scary. But, as it is your story, you can be creative and tell the story you want to write.

For a children's story, no matter for what age, you should consider the minimum number of characters. Don't introduce characters unless they have a real purpose in your story, so ensure characters are justified. Make sure each character adds to the story and makes it move forward.

How long should your story be for the children you are writing for? As usual with writing, particularly fiction, the answer lies somewhere around the perfect mark – as long as it takes to tell the story, not a word more, not a line less. But don't make it an epic novel. Keep it to a reasonable length. Don't write the children's version of *War and Peace*. Your readers will sure fall asleep and enjoy a good night's sleep, brought on, of course, by boredom.

In your story, something should always be happening, or about to happen. Endless descriptions for the sake of describing something are not required here. Include those descriptions in the dialogue, through actions, through feelings whenever possible. Always show, don't tell the readers what is happening or why, or the way people feel. Always show them the emotions of others.

A good writer's role through writing children's literature is to instil positive qualities in the characters, or at least the main characters. Of course, a villain would not have many positive qualities, but you can show the positive qualities in the children when they overcome evil, or outsmart the villain. But always bring in action – action with something falling to pieces, action through a dog running through the woods.

As children are usually happy young people, humour is always welcome in children's literature. Make the children laugh. Make them smile. Let them see that the world really is a fun place to live in and that they are very much a part of the fun. Try to include the children as characters doing something that is funny or outrageous, but don't decide to be nasty in the process of being funny at someone else's expense.

The ending must be happy too, and positive, with a positive message that the readers can go to bed on, and feel relaxed and satisfied that something good came of the story they have just enjoyed, or have had read to them while they were tucked into bed at night.

To be a children's writer, you must understand the minds of the children for whom you are writing, and the way their minds work for that particular age group. It is not sufficient to say, 'okay, I am going to write a story for children, so here goes.' It won't go, and that approach won't get you very far.

Children of different age groups face very different problems, different ethical and cultural and moral issues. You have to understand the mind of the age group you want to write for.

Little known facts, and little known facets of life can be introduced through children's literature.

Many children want to be shown the difference between right and wrong, between good and bad. And they want to be shown these aspects of life in a fresh, interesting and revealing way. Don't lecture to them. They don't want to feel guilty about something they might be doing, or feel they are the cause of something in their lives they are going through, perhaps with their parents or with friends. They don't want to think they might be the cause of the breakdown of their parents' relationship.

Children's stories can be divided into four main groups — books for the under-five year old readers, those between five years of age up to a reading age of about seven years, eight years up to eleven years, and young adult from about twelve years reading age to mid-teens.

YOUNG READERS

Let's look at what goes into the first group — writing for the under-five year olds. Most books for this age group will be picture books, with little or no text, perhaps just single words. This sounds simple, doesn't it? It's not!

Most children in this age group are very happy, and they don't take life too seriously. A good children's author can be as creative as he or she likes — the more so, the better.

Books for this age group can be about anything within reason, but within the 'reasonable' part, there are definitely a few no-no subjects and approaches.

A young mind might enjoy a story about something they can relate to, something in their environment, such as a wild animal (but perhaps not too wild!), some insects, a colony of ants, or even going shopping with their grandparents. Tell them what the child did, what they saw, what they bought, how they enjoyed it. Keep it simple, but keep it interesting.

You might come up with several ideas to begin with, but pick the theme of the book you want to write. With all the ideas for possible books, one will stand out from all the others. This is the one to choose.

If you put your story on the beach, don't make the description of the water or the sand take over the whole book. You could concentrate on the creepy-crawly things in the rock pools, such as the octopus a child might see there, or perhaps the small fish.

With books catering for this young age group, the emphasis will not be so much on character development or scene or plot. You will describe the activities, perhaps through the child's eyes, or through the eyes of an adult the child could relate to.

For readers of this young age group, everything must be visual. You will need to build up the scene, and you will need lots of illustrations to get the readers' attention and to keep it. If you can't keep the child's attention going past the first couple of pages, you have lost that child, and you can be sure the parents and the grandparents will not bother buying the second book you write.

THE NEXT AGE GROUP OF YOUNG READERS
The second group of children's books will be different from the first group.

With books catering for five- to seven-year-old readers, you can use a lot more text and fewer illustrations. Even a children's novel will need illustrations just to lift the story, and to keep the child's interest. A child's mind can create lots of images, and even a simple illustration or two scattered throughout the book will help the child create images more vividly.

The story for this age group can relate to something the

child is familiar with, such as real-life situations but in a pleasing way, or something creative the child can relate to.

It could be the story of a child who wants to earn some money to buy himself a bicycle, and he gets a job working for a small private zoo. This would be totally fiction of course, but the child could take on a more important role than other children would be able to. They might need someone they can look up to. It could describe the characters' interactions with the animals, and with the other staff at the zoo. You could throw in other elements, such as an approaching bushfire. But make sure the zoo is saved. None of the animals will be allowed to suffer. Children usually love animals, and the last thing they want to do is to see their beloved animals harmed in any way. So any extraneous factor must have a happy outcome, one that could possibly lead to other successes later in the story.

In a longer story for this age group, you could build up the main character throughout the story. Don't tell your readers what the character is like all at once on the first page. Let you readers imagine that person you are describing, and let the readers add bits to their image of him and help them build up their own picture.

Any act of heroism or outstanding behaviour must be shown to the readers. It is not sufficient merely to tell readers that he was brave. You must show how he was brave, and how the actions stood out from what would normally be expected from a person in that situation — how he saved the zoo from the bushfire, or how he extracted the cow from the tangled fence, despite the nearby bulls looking on and trying to protect the cow.

But like all fiction, you story will be just that — made up

by you and a creation of your own, the author.

Other themes for children's books catering for readers in this group could be shown through observations of everyday life. Even a typical, everyday incident in our lives, or more correctly, the lives of young people, is an important theme for a young mind.

For books catering for this age group, the style will be different from those written for children under five years of age. Your characters can be more involved, and more involved with those around them. You can use longer words, and use sentences that are more complex. Children in the age group of readers enjoy fantasy, and science fiction. Children have very vivid imaginations, and become involved in the stories they are reading. Write for that age group, and make sure you do not write down to them. That means keeping the style consistent with what readers in this age group would understand and expect. On the other hand, don't use words or expressions beyond their reasonable comprehension. The readers must be able to understand what you have written, to be able to enjoy the book, and get some satisfaction and enjoyment from reading it.

EIGHT- TO ELEVEN-YEAR-OLD READERS

For eight-year old to around the eleven-year-old readers, the types of books would be different again. Children in this age group will be looking for a more involved story, with fewer illustrations, and more intrigue. Longer words could be used, within reason.

TWELVE YEARS TO YOUNG ADULT READERS

Readers in this age group of twelve years to young adult need something that is different from all the previous groups. They will be more mature, and be getting a better grip on life, not as it is, but as it should be. So this could include stories of families, and of their problems, and their relationship to their friends, or how their enemies at school make life difficult for them. But make sure that the families survive any crisis in your story, because your young readers will want a happy outcome. Their own parents might be fighting out their demons, but the child wants to think that there is hope for their family. Their own family is extremely important to them at that age, and that could even include their own life. Give them hope. Show through a positive message that not all is lost in their world, and that by taking a different direction occasionally, different results can occur.

Even for this age group, the stories should be visual, so use plenty of vivid descriptions, and plenty of emotion. But show the emotion, don't tell the readers that someone was unhappy — show how they were depressed, and why. If you show them why someone was depressed, they should be able to put themselves in that person's place and experience the emotion themselves. That is one reason why it is important to give the readers a positive outcome with a good-news story at the end to leave the young mind in a positive mood.

Just as you would when writing fiction for adults, you would need to include the beginning and the middle. The end of course is where everything in the story comes together and brings in the happy resolution that leaves the young readers with something nice to think about after they have put down the book.

Illustrations will help to break down the pages and pages of text, and will help to lift the story somewhat.

CONSIDER OTHER FAMILIES

For stories in any of these categories you are interested in writing about, discuss with other parents what their children might be interested in, and what types of themes would interest them most.

Also discuss with the children themselves if you have a chance, perhaps those attending a daycare centre, or other group you are involved in. What do they enjoy? You might be able to read stories to small groups to assess their reactions to different stories. If you get no reaction, they obviously haven't been listening. And why haven't they been listening? It's probably because the story was boring.

If you get a lot of interaction from the children or from their parents, they obviously enjoyed one story over several others, so use that to guide you in what you might want to write about.

ILLUSTRATIONS

Can you illustrate a children's book? If you can, you are ahead of many writers who want to write for children. You can create the images that you want, to fit into the book at the places throughout where you want them to be placed, without having to rely on someone else's interpretation of what you have in mind.

Many creative people are talented in more that one area, so is it possible you could illustrate your own children's books? Pencil or pen drawings work well.

If not, there are two options. Employ the services of a good artist who can illustrate the book. The artist must be able to provide you with the illustrations you ask for, and deliver them within a reasonable time. You don't want to wait three years before you get the first illustration, and find that it is not anything like the one you had in mind for your story.

There is some very good drawing software on the market these days, and you might consider using one of these products to create the pictures you want. A picture on the computer is built up bit by little bit, a stroke of the 'brush' to suit your theme, followed by another stroke of a 'brush' with perhaps another shade for good effect.

Using such software is itself challenging and allows you to be creative, and if you can succeed here, you might be pleasantly surprised at the pictures you create.

The last option for illustrations is to search the Internet for artists who could illustrate your book for you. You would need to supply a copy of the text, and a brief of exactly what you want, and which illustrations you want to go where in your story.

If you go with this option, get a firm quote on price per illustration. Stipulate a completion date for the project. And make sure the artist realises that the completion date and the price are firm — with no flexibility, and no add-ons after the work is completed.

Of course, you might have to pay the artist a royalty fee for each copy of the book you sell, and you should include the artist in the process — Written by Me, Illustrated by Her.

BOOK FORMAT

Decide on the format of the book you envisage even before you begin creating the illustrations — will your book be A4 portrait size, A4 landscape, or some other size?

You cannot create a small image to fit an A5 publication (that's half of an A4 book) and expect to increase the size of the illustrations. The result will be blocky, or pixilated, and if you dared to use it, your readers will certainly be disappointed with the whole effect of the finished book.

For younger children, and the very young, the font should be quite large. As you write for older children, the size of the font can be reduced, so that when you are writing for say twelve-year-olds, you could use a Times New Roman twelve point or similar.

PUBLISHING YOUR OWN BOOK

Now for the good news and the bad news.

About twenty-five years to thirty years ago, many publishers started going out of children's books. And over about the next five years, many publishers stopped publishing children's books altogether.

Others would publish only the old stories — Enid Blyton's books for example. They realised that parents and particularly grandparents bought books for the children, and they would buy books that they had enjoyed as a child. And why not? If they liked an author, or a story or an adventure, they could reasonably assume that the child they were buying the book for would also like the same book. So in the end, bookshops contained books by the well-known writers from an earlier time, seldom a newer author.

That was nearly thirty years ago. And everything has changed yet again.

Many publishers no longer exist. Others have been swallowed up by bigger publishers who in turn have disappeared into the bowels of even bigger publishers. Now there is no competition, and not many opportunities to publish the number of books that are written every year. Some authors have their work published, but many are not so lucky.

The good news is that with the demise of so many publishers around the world, and with the demise of so many bookshops around the world too, authors tend to think that opportunities to have a book by a new author published are extremely limited.

But not so. Think in terms of self-publishing, and I have included a chapter on self-publishing further along in this book.

I believe self-publishing for any book is now the way to go for many authors, particularly new authors, and those trying to break into the field of writing.

The opportunities to self-publish are limited by your personal resources, and by the energy you are prepared to put into the marketing of your book.

The days when you could get your book published by a mainstream publisher, and wait for the royalty cheque to arrive every six months, are over.

Even back thirty or more years ago there were many problems for writers. Often the cheque didn't arrive. Many times their books would be remaindered (or sold off at cost-price after six months). The days when a writer could submit their proposal to one of perhaps six publishers and wait for one of them to accept the work are over. Publishers did go through a phase where they would only work with literary agents. The role of the literary agent was to sift out the good from the less than good manuscripts and forward only a small number of excellent works on to the publishers. Even that procedure is no longer used, because there are so few publishers.

In those days of long ago (at least in publishing terms), authors still had to market their own book, because most publishers would maintain an interest in individual books, and in individual authors, for only a very short time. Other books were being published all the time, and each of those would need attention too.

Enter now the realm of the self-publisher. In the 'old days' this would have been known as vanity press, or vanity publishing, but now it is regarded as a legitimate and acceptable way to have new books brought onto the market. Some writers have done very well by publishing books themselves, and the success with children's books are no exception.

Maybe you will become the next best-selling author of children's books. I hope so!

Chapter 9 Writing Articles For Magazines

In this chapter, I will show you the craft of writing articles for magazines. You will learn how to get ideas and develop them, and the craft of editing. Learn how to build on your experiences. After you have written and have had published several articles, you will develop confidence in writing, and above all, you should develop a real desire to write articles, and enjoyment in doing so.

An important part of writing articles for magazines, and increasing your payments for your work, is to rework those articles with a different slant or with a different reader in mind for other magazines by offering different publishing rights.

But the real benefits will come from writing, and lots of it.

What is writing for magazines all about? It is the sharing of information, experiences and knowledge, with others. Your opinions are an important part of the subject for any magazine article. You can write about how you see something, how you feel about it, or understand it. Your personality gives interest to your writing. People enjoy sharing feelings. That's why social media is so popular. They will enjoy reading about how you see something, how you relate to the world in a way that might even help them in a time of difficulty.

Interest lies not so much in the topic as in what you have done with that topic. An interesting subject can be made boring by bad writing, whereas an otherwise ordinary subject can have life breathed into it by good writing.

Purpose means the effect you want to have on your readers. While all these points may enter a particular piece of writing, one will usually predominate and determine the basic direction of the writing. Whether it succeeds or fails will depend on how much thought you have given to your readers.

Although the purpose of writing is to convey information, your primary duty as a writer is to convey that information in such a way that it is easily understood by all your readers. A magazine article, however, is no place to air grievances or to complain.

Financial rewards from writing for magazines can be determined by how much time you are prepared to contribute to your projects. Payments for articles are influenced by a number of other factors, including the sales of a magazine, the print run, the income received from advertising. Payment to you, the writer, can be reduced if the editor has to spend a lot of time reworking your article. Payment could be more if your article is good enough to be published with little or no editing. Payments for a typical article that includes three or four accompanying photographs could double that received for the writing alone. Occasionally articles attract no payment. The fine print of many magazines might include a clause that says something like 'payment is at the discretion of the editor'. Unfortunately, some editors use their discretion in a creative way and choose not to pay contributors. The magazine might have such colossal overheads, huge staff salaries to meet, printing costs, and be top-heavy, and there really is no money to pay contributors. Unfortunately, these same editors seem to forget that without good contributors, they simply wouldn't have a good magazine to produce. In that case, put it down to experience, and move on to the next magazine article. If the magazine that published your work is one of reasonable quality, you can use that to your advantage. I'll show you how to do that a little later.

Always be interested in writing (you will write much better) and be very interested in what you are writing about. Your writing will certainly reflect this level of interest. Consider whether it is really worth the three hundred dollars or so for those hours (or days) of uninspiring boredom while you write something that does not interest you. Few people have the personal resources to excel at something that is of little or no interest to stimulate them.

I have mentioned elsewhere the real value of the writers notebook. For writing articles, this will be valuable. The notebook does not have to be a large, heavy book. Something small, perhaps one that can fit comfortably into the top pocket or handbag will be suitable for jotting down ideas. Keep a writers notebook with you at all times so you can write down any ideas, even phrases, that come to you during your activities. Keep it accessible even while you are writing an article. Soon the notebook will contain ideas that could be used in the current article, or ideas that could be developed in the future. You could eventually come to consider that nearly every good entry in your notebook could be the source of several hundred dollars — one good idea, one good payment. That alone should be enough to encourage you to carry such a notebook.

Tenacity, never taking no from editors, but being ever critical of their own work contributes to a writer's success. This is what is going to enable you to write successfully for magazines.

As a writer, always aim to make the next article better than the last one you wrote. Even with only a slight improvement each time, your style of writing will improve markedly. Look back after a while to check your progress. If you think your first few were terrible, perhaps you may even be embarrassed by reading them, then you truly have made progress. And this will show that you can judge your own work more critically after you have gained experience and confidence.

What constitutes a publishable article? Just because it is returned from editors, does that mean your article is unpublishable? No, it certainly does not. Consider that miserable editor who is having a dreadful day because of any number of reasons. Look for a more suitable market, or a better time to submit it.

What is the best time to submit articles? Cynically, it is easy to say just before the topic you have chosen has become popular, so that you can get your article published ahead of the others that will be submitted to editors. In reality, keep looking for possible themes in life, themes in government, trends, social issues. Try to keep at least even with them. But this does not mean that you could not be experimental in your writing.

THE EDITOR

Choose a magazine. Any magazine will do. What does the editor want? You can judge this to a greater or lesser degree by reading a range of articles the editor has published. Does the editor want variety for the readers? Do all articles read more or less the same, in style, length and subject? Then satisfy the editor's needs and, through that person, your readers. Editors know their readers.

Surveys are carried out from time to time to determine a reader profile, including what is his occupation, how much does he earn, does he have a family, own a washing machine, how many television sets does the household possess, when did he last go on holidays, or overseas? While some of these surveys are carried out for advertising purposes, they also give a clear profile of who the readers are, what they like, what their interests are, and so on.

Often surveys will be conducted by a magazine, and a form included with a particular issue. If you receive one, complete it. It will help the editor, and through him, the writers, to tailor articles to more popular types of writing and subjects. Often, the editor really is trying to find out what readers want each issue. Tastes change. People change. And so your articles must change to keep pace with the readers, and with their expectations.

To a writer, the editor is just as important as the readers. You must first of all convince the editor of the soundness of your idea, convince him of your ability to write about the subject you propose, and that you are indeed the ideal person to write the article for his magazine.

But never forget that the editor is human. Many writers hold the editor up as some mysterious figure who is unapproachable, one who only says no to the material they write. The editor, like yourself, has feelings, has emotions, and gets rather annoyed when a writer contributes material that is quite unsuitable for that particular publication. But wouldn't we all feel that way if we were inundated with inappropriate time-wasting material that we have to read through and consider? I am sure we would.

An editor's role is to select, from the vast array of articles and submissions received, those that are most appropriate to the magazine. He will probably ask himself, 'Have my readers read enough about this?' 'What's new in this article?' 'Is it well written?' 'Would my readers like to read this?' 'How will they react to it?' In other words, 'is this what my readers would like to read?' 'Is it suitable?' 'Is it accurate?' 'Would it require a lot of my time if I were to accept it for publication?'

Plan your work well ahead to meet editors' deadlines, but never expect your article to be published in the next issue of any magazine. It might be. But often editors plan several issues ahead, which could mean a delay of several months before you see your work in print. But one thing that will speed up the publication of your article is if it is well written, requires no editing, and is accompanied by several really great photographs, properly edited or cropped, that match the subject of your article perfectly. Then, on the magazine's deadline, and if your editor has a hundred articles he is planning on reworking to suit his magazine, and is in need of just one more story, yours will have a good chance of being published in the next issue. Now wouldn't that be great? But remember, your article must be first-class, requiring no editorial work on it. In other words, your article must be just about perfect. The good thing about writing is that it really doesn't take much longer to write a very good article than it does to write something that is below standard for most magazines. It can easily be refined in the editing stage.

PRESENTATION

Let us now look at an important aspect of writing — the presentation of your manuscript

Proper presentation goes a long way to getting a favourable response from an editor. We will look at some of the ways in which your article can be enhanced so that the desired response from an editor is more likely.

Always be professional in your approach, in your attitude to your writing, and to the manuscripts you submit. Your manuscript should always reflect your expertise as a writer and your authority on your subject. Neatness counts for everything these days.

Your page should have wide margins at the top, bottom, and on both sides. Leave at least 1 inch (2.5 centimetre) margins all around. This is not just to make the article look neater, it is so the editor can make corrections, give the production staff instructions for typesetting your article, and scribble any other notes and additional information that may be considered necessary to get the article ready for publishing. Some would also add to this list, so the editor can write his facetious comments on the copy. You will most likely send the article to the editor by email, so make sure it is in a format used by most computers, such as Microsoft Word – a reasonably late version too. If you are emailing the article, send a list of photographs and captions, mark the photographs so they can be matched up with the page of captions (each photograph will have a number, so use it), and send the photographs on the one email as attachments – never put them on a page.

Use double spacing between lines. Again, this is so the editor can make any corrections or changes to the copy you have submitted. It gives the editor more room to move on your page if your article is accepted.

Correct spelling is important, so use a dictionary or the spell check of your computer. Beware of the pitfalls and the limitations of computer spell checks, though. They have an inability to differentiate between similar words, for example 'to', 'too' and 'two', or 'they're' and 'there', 'threw' and 'through', 'there' and 'their'.

Always use good quality A4 size 80 gsm bond sheets of paper if you are using snail mail. This is the international standard paper size, and is preferred by editors. By using heavier grade of paper, the text from the next page won't show through the one the editor is trying to read.

COPYRIGHT

Unless the writer has entered into an agreement with a magazine or journal early in the writing, the writer owns the copyright, although this can vary from country to country, and is reviewed from time to time. So if you own the copyright for an article you are writing today, different rules regarding the copyright of the articles you write in the coming years might apply. An exception to this rule is the printing of works in publications owned by Australian State or the Federal governments. In such cases, the copyright transfers to the Crown.

By retaining copyright, you, as author, can submit the same work to other magazines. The next article then becomes second publishing rights or even third or fourth publishing rights, but let the editor know that it has been previously published. You can reuse any part of it in another form. In other words, if you retain copyright, the article is yours to do as you wish with it.

When you retain copyright, unless you enter into an arrangement with a publisher, you are free to sell the article elsewhere, or even adapt it for another media. Some moral considerations are important. First, if you submit a published article to another magazine, do not include any editorial changes made by the first editor who published it. Do not take the credit for that editor's work in making your work better.

RESEARCH

Where do you look for the information you need? Newspapers often are not detailed, and not relevant except perhaps for researching historic articles. Many journal articles are written by specialists, and are refereed. That is, one or two specialists in that particular subject will check every article published for accuracy before it goes into print.

Many authors write books on subjects of their expertise, as well as writing journal articles. Never discount the use of books for reference purposes. Sometimes old books are ideal for research, such as research on the wars. Learn how to use your library to obtain the information you require.

The source of information for writers is available on almost every computer. It's called the Internet. Since its introduction, the world wide web has expanded at an astonishing rate to provide source material on almost every imaginable subject, and many subjects that one could not even imagine. Of course, this does not mean that you take material straight from the Internet, put your name on it and hope it will be published. That's not what writing is about at all, so don't do it. Please! If you are connected to the Internet, use it. If you are not connected, inquire about a low-cost service provider, get an email address, and start searching your topics. Most topics on the Internet are very recent, many are updated frequently, and may become available even before they are published in journals.

DISPATCHING YOUR ARTICLE

The title should be centred, with sub-headings left-aligned and in a smaller font than the title. Leave an extra space between each section (before the sub-headings). If a sub-heading appears on the bottom of the page and the text of that section begins on the next page, push the sub-heading over to the next page. Headings on one page and the text on the next look sloppy. And don't forget to add your name under the title. Your contact details, including your name again, should go on a covering sheet attached to the manuscript. Use either a ten-point or twelve-point font throughout. Headings should be the same size as the body text, but can be put in bold type.

Not all computer programs convert simply. Often punctuation, indenting, and other attributes are deleted, but if provided in plain text, tidying up the text is usually no problem. The production team at the magazine will enhance the text into its finished magazine page format. Even if you have the software to provide the article in the same program as that used by the magazine, do not do any of the formatting, such as arranging the text in three columns, or leaving large spaces for illustrations. The production staff will do that in the style they have selected, with background, headings, font (type face) and page format that are used by that magazine.

If in your final reading of the article before posting it or emailing it, you need to make small changes on a single page, ensure that reworking that page does not affect the following page. Make sure that that page begins and ends with the same words as before, or print out the subsequent page or pages too.

Every page must be numbered — even if you submit the material electronically.

If you are dispatching your article by snail mail rather than by email, use a paper clip to hold the pages together in their correct order. This makes it easy for production staff to work on one page at a time, without the need to bend pages over.

Send the article, illustrations and computer disk flat in an A4 envelope.

The good news is that many magazines now prefer electronic submission of manuscripts. This saves on postage, is quicker, and you don't need to worry about sending disks with your work. Photographs can also be submitted electronically, usually as JPEG files, with a minimum of 300 dpi resolution. But check with the editor how he or she requires them.

If you follow these instructions, your manuscript should reflect your expertise as a writer and your professionalism on your subject. The appearance of your manuscript will tell the editor a lot about yourself.

BECOMING AN EXPERT

Once you have had several articles published, use your portfolio of writing successes to get many more articles accepted by editors. Experience opens up other writing opportunities for those who know how to make the most use of their portfolio. Quote even those you had published without payment. If the magazine is one of reasonable quality, it will make the editor feel that someone else believed that your work was good enough to publish. And that's a real contribution to your success.

Become an expert in your chosen field and make your work snowball. Use one article and your experience to get the next editor's acceptance of other articles.

Assume an air of confidence and experience in all query letters. When you send out a query letter, it is beneficial to say that you have had articles published in several magazines on a similar subject (and quote the magazine titles).

Let's get started. You're now going to think about all the subjects that interest you, and all aspects of each of those topics that you can write about. Then we will look at magazines that will want your articles.

GETTING IDEAS

Most writers, when they begin, find this part the most difficult for showing any reasonable progress. It sounds easy, but often it is not. So we will get a lot of the essential hard work over early.

Few writers can sit at a computer and say, 'I am going to write an article ... let me see ... I'll write one about ...' Yet, with concentration, you will be surprised at how many potential ideas you have, how many points of view about each subject you can think of, and just what else you would like to write about and ideas you can share with others.

Ideas for potential articles are all around you. Examples include a profile of the life of a retired radio presenter, bringing up a difficult child, unusual work practices you know of that may be valuable to others, an interesting lifestyle you know of, interesting work or an unusual hobby, perhaps something for the home or a craft item you have created.

You might have worked on a farm. You will have lots of ideas from that experience. Anything that is going to make a farmer's life easier will be appreciated. Farming magazines would be receptive to good ideas. Topics could be time management on the farm, the benefits of share farming, to spray or not to spray (an interesting one because of the stupid laws regarding what is an approved spray and what isn't). Some magazines cater for the city farmers, many of whom are looking for good ideas and new methods that lifetime farmers take for granted. You could also look at innovations in farming.

Anxiety and depression are widely suffered in just about any community, but few people realise the full significance of what this means to others. A general view of what it means to suffer from depression, how it holds the person back, how, like many other illnesses of this type, it alienates the sufferer from work, friends and family, would make interesting reading. A possible market for this type of article could be a magazine that publishes 'this is what it's like' stories.

Other angles could include 'how effective is modern treatment for this type of illness?' 'Are there miracle cures for depression?' 'Will there be breakthroughs in the near future?' 'What's it like to depend on medication for long periods?' 'How do you get back into society?' (include a variety of viewpoints here).

An interesting article could be how treatment for this type of condition has improved (or not improved despite improvements in other areas of mental health). For some of these angles, Saturday supplements of newspapers could be worth exploring. And what about one from a personal viewpoint about the 'five-star' accommodation at the hospitals?

Belief (as in very strong confidence in one's ability or talents, or an overwhelming desire to achieve a goal), will point others in the right direction to self-achievement and self-fulfilment. Look at the effectiveness of determination and belief in oneself to reach personal goals.

Possible markets here could be well-being magazines (for the effectiveness of belief). Motivation magazines (there are quite a few published in the United States of America on this subject) would be appropriate for articles on the effectiveness of determination and belief in goals.

Health and fitness: an article on quitting smoking could be humorous. You could also dwell on the belief and determination aspects, and bring that into this topic as well. The idea of relaxation is good, and important. List some of the benefits that relaxation can achieve, both in its own right, and as an adjunct to other personal goals, such as using relaxation coupled with creative visualisation to achieve personal development, to feel better and to handle anxiety and even relationships better.

You might have enjoyed public speaking during your working life. The public speaking idea would be appropriate in magazines such as those catering for personal development and management (often managers give dreadful presentations, so anything that would appeal to managers would appeal to editors of those magazines). A 'believe in what you say' angle is appropriate, but could I suggest that you tell readers that 'if you don't believe in what you say, who else is going to believe you?' How to give a dynamic presentation, how to overcome nervousness, how to feel good about giving a presentation, or public speaking.

In addition to these subjects, you also have potential subjects you might not be aware of.

The door-to-door experience you had as a salesman could be good for at least two articles. One possibly humorous article about some of the questions and the expectations of your prospective customers might lift a reader's spirits. One of the in-flight airline magazines might like the humorous one on this topic. But other angles could include 'how I increased my sales quota' (a self-imposed quota, as in setting goals), what does it take to get started as a salesperson (suitable for magazines catering for those seeking opportunities). This could also be brought into an article written for those who are setting up their own business. What do they need to know about selling before they go into business?

Your resume might have gaps in it. Ask around, and write an article on how people fill gaps in their work history. This could be a very humorous story, and would be suitable for magazines on management (telling managers how applicants fudge their data), and another article from the perspective of applicants who come up with some rather unusual stories to overcome gaps in their work histories.

Listen for ideas, in conversation, in the news, on television, in magazines, in fact almost everywhere. That's where a writer's notebook will be beneficial. Write down all the things that you may want to write about. Your notebook stores perceptions, ideas, emotions, actions. All these provide material for articles.

An idea is merely just that. The next step is to develop that idea, explore the idea. Everyone has plenty to write about.

DIVERSIFY YOUR TOPICS

It's often far more interesting writing about several completely different topics rather than concentrating on one rather narrow field. Other writers prefer to concentrate on one, maybe two topics they know well. If you know your subjects well, you can write the articles faster than if you must spend much of your potential writing time researching each topic. If you concentrate on a rather narrow range of topics, you could find that you exhaust them after a few articles. It is embarrassing to tell editors that you have written a series of articles for several magazines about welding topics, and then approach another editor and tell him that you now want to write an article about growing trees on farms. What is the connection? What is the relevance of one topic to the next.

Don't hang on the one theme that every other writer has chosen, such as AIDS or domestic violence. These themes have been written into the grave already. If you need to write about them, you must take a fresh angle. New information you are able to provide, or new ideas you have, could make the article more interesting, or appeal to new readers. But most likely, such topics would have comatosed more than one reader of more than one magazine already.

Be prepared to take opposing views where appropriate, such as how dangerous the natural world is, with its naturally occurring toxins and deadly plant chemicals, and arsenic, asbestos, silica and diatomaceous earths. Remember that you have plenty to write about, otherwise you wouldn't want to become a writer!

LOOK FOR A SLANT

The next thing to look at with writing for magazines is to see how many different slants you can come up with for the one topic. This is an example, so draw up your own lists and see just how many different slants you can create. It's all up to your imagination! The idea of this exercise is

Subject	Point of view	Possible markets
Welding		
	Safety	
	Home projects	
	Farm welding	
	Setting up a workshop	
	Repairs around the home	
	Repairs on the farm	
	Repairing cast iron	
	Welding sheet steel	
	An introduction to welding	
	Equipment you will need	
	Car repairs using a welder	
	Making wrought-iron gates	
	Swimming pool fences	
	Making a bull bar	
	Wrought-iron railing	
Bus shelter artwork		
	Juvenile art	
	Municipal interest	
	Community art projects	
	Preventing delinquency	
	Achievements by students	

to list all the topics that interest you. The first task is to list the broad topics, such as a craft, the next might be farming, the third might be computers, the next might be metalwork, and so on.

The next task is to break each of those subjects down as much as possible. List every aspect of each main heading that you can possibly think of. So the first, say welding, might include setting up a welding workshop; the second, welding safety; the third, home projects; the fourth, farm welding; the fifth, welding repairs, and so on.

The table on the opposite page shows the rough breakdown of a couple of subjects. You might prefer to work with a similar table, or you may wish to use a separate sheet of paper for each general topic. Whichever is your preferred choice, leave a column on the right for the next part of this exercise.

The main thing now is to list as many topics, and treatments of those topics, as you can. But remember that you should never consider the table as finite. Always add subjects, treatments, points of view to it whenever you can. This is where you will benefit from carrying around with you a small notebook, so any flashes that come to you can be recorded before they are lost forever. Keep the lists open, and see how often you can add to them. Sometimes ideas will come to a dead end. That's alright, just accept it. But if you think that each entry could mean a payment of, say, $300, I am sure that that alone will be a good incentive to expand that list.

Remember, the more subjects you can list, and the more angles you can think of, the better. Even if they sound silly at the time, you may be surprised at how even these can be modified, toned down slightly, and turned into a very readable article. It is often the different aspects that people want to read about.

The table is an example of what your own table could look like.

Lists such as these could go on and on. But by now you will have a good idea of what you will be compiling. Leave the third column blank for now. You will be filling that out shortly.

Your task now is to compile your own list.

MATCHING YOUR IDEAS TO MARKETS

Match potential markets, or magazines, to those topics you listed in your table. It may seem strange listing more than one magazine against each treatment, but you will realise that more than one magazine could be interested in a topic. It's called working smarter, not harder. By reusing your material, you will cut down your research time, and increase your profits from writing even further.

To select a magazine that might be interested in buying your article, browse through a range of magazines covering related topics at your newsagent. Larger libraries carry a range of magazines in their holdings. Directories such as the *Australian Writers Marketplace*, and equivalent writers guides that are published for the benefits of writers in America, New Zealand and just about everywhere else are excellent sources of potential magazines for your articles. Most magazines have details of the publisher, production staff and the name of the editor, and address and other contact details. You will need this information. Many such directories will give details of submission requirements, the format the editor prefers, whether a query letter is wanted, and other relevant information for each magazine.

Consider the artwork that is painted in the bus shelters and on exterior walls of public buildings in some cities and towns. Over many years now, community groups and school students have been encouraged to decorate the walls of public buildings with works of art. Some councils are even encouraging school art students to decorate the exterior walls of public toilets with colourful murals to enhance their aesthetics. It works, so this type of work (as distinct from graffiti, which is also paining on toilet walls) should be encouraged. Most of it enhances the otherwise drab concrete walls of the shelters and toilet blocks, and has significantly reduced vandalism in those public areas. This subject in itself may not seem too exciting to most writers, but think about it for a moment. Who would be interested in reading about such a subject? Lots of people!

Possible readers would include school counsellors and municipal council workers: school counsellors because the students are given, indeed encouraged, to take on a community role, and municipal council workers because it shows council staff that there really is local community spirit. The same subject would be of interest to readers of police magazines as it would show how juvenile art can be used to reduce delinquency or vandalism. The same subject in children's publications would illustrate achievements and community activity and attitudes. Readers of bus and transport magazines could find the topic of interest in enhancing the facilities that are provided for patrons. School magazines, as well as magazines covering community arts programs could be interested in publishing such material to illustrate new forms and venues for artistic talents.

The table will now show how to break down broad topics to specific treatments, and allocate potential magazines to each. Your next task is to consider magazines against each of the topics and angles you listed. Your table now will have (1) subject, (2) aspect or point of view or treatment, and (3) magazines that would be interested in those treatments.

Now you can get started on the first article. So let's approach the first editor.

THE QUERY LETTER

Find suitable magazines that could be interested in your proposed article, but approach one editor at a time. You would be embarrassed if six of them wanted the same article.

There are two thoughts about when you should send off a query letter — before you even begin to write, so that you can be guided by any particular points that the editor wants you to include, or after you have at least begun the article and perhaps written the first draft, so that you know that you have an article.

On the second point, it is surprising how many writers begin with a good idea, only to find after many hours (or, sometimes, days), that there really isn't an article in their idea after all. I prefer to send the query letter first, so I don't have to write an article that is not going anywhere. But you will get a feel for what is right for you.

Make sure the contact details are current. Editors change frequently. Even if you have the latest edition of a magazine, it is often advisable to ring the magazine and ask if Mr or Ms So-and-so is the editor. An electronic query to the editor these days is usually acceptable. Send an email with an outline of your proposed article, especially if that approach is recommended in the magazine.

Here is an example of a query letter for an article you want to write about the use of fodder trees on farms.

And that is all there is to a query letter. In it, you are stating your wish to write such an article, why you feel it is important, and you are telling the editor that you are quite capable of writing it. Keep it brief.

The next step is up to the editor, so it is your job, as a writer, to convince him that the article you propose is ideal for his readers.

Modify this letter, of course, to suit the magazine you have chosen, your topic, and your approach.

Of course, if you are sending an email query, just give the substance of this letter, not the address of the magazine, nor should you address the email to 'Dear Editor.' In an email, include your telephone number in case the editor wants to discuss the article with you — and perhaps even ask you to write a series of articles on a common subject. Yes, this does occasionally happen.

"I am writing an article entitled *The use of fodder trees for livestock production in Australia*. In it I am showing the historical use of trees as a source of feed for stock, but I am concentrating on their use in Australia. In Australia, we have tremendous potential for the use of such trees, but so far little use has been made of their potential compared with other countries.

I expect the article to run to about 2000 words. I could let you have the finished article within four weeks.

Would you like to receive my completed article *The Use of Fodder Trees For Livestock Production in Australia?*"

Harry Greentrees

BREAKING YOUR ARTICLE DOWN

It is difficult to work at a computer, and after a couple of hours, complete an article that is tidy, structured in an orderly fashion, and saying just what the writer wanted, without any thought going into the planning.

Even more often, writers sit in front of a computer for hours without producing anything at all. It is called writers block, is very common, and, I think, is caused by the enormity of the task ahead of them.

Often ideas and points of view are generated merely by jotting down as quickly as you can all ideas on a topic that come to you.

One way (but there may be other ways that are just as effective) is to break down a large task into a number of smaller components.

Writing two thousand words about unemployment might be considered a huge task.

But could you write one hundred words about how easy it was to get a job twenty-five years ago? One hundred words is a small amount of work, so quite possibly you would answer yes to this question.

Could you write one hundred words about how easy it was twenty-five years ago to get a job if the applicant had a degree? Yes, of course you could!

And another hundred words on how difficult it is now to get a job if the applicant has one degree? Of course you can. There are probably examples of young graduates all around you. Just ask your relatives and friends!

So we are starting to break down two thousand words into manageable blocks. Keep doing this until you have exhausted all the areas you wish to cover in your article.

These headings will form an outline of your proposed article. An outline is usually necessary, but many writers let their writing just evolve and they tidy up the result at the end. But in the early stages of writing articles, I suggest you use headings and sub-headings, or minor headings, and lots of them. Sub-headings will make the task of writing more organised and easier. These can be removed later if you no longer need them. Also they serve as a guide to even the work out over a number of points rather than concentrating on one point more than the others. Headings make it easier to write the article, as they break down the psychological barriers to writing. You will realise you need to write one hundred words about twenty related topics, rather than two thousand words about one subject. They also break up the block of text for the readers.

Without worrying about their order, go over your jottings, keeping any that are promising and discarding those that are not. Not all the points you thought of for a particular subject will be useful, so what do you leave out? The answer is, everything that is not related to that angle you want to take. But importantly, what new points can you raise in your argument? Most readers don't want to read a rewrite of someone else's ideas. Your point of view must be fresh.

But for now, we'll work only with headings. So write down every point that you think might be important to your article. The list might seem a mess, but it is important at this stage to at least get those points listed.

The next task is to arrange each of those subjects in a logical order, and one that will make your ideas flow smoothly without jumping from one area, back to another that should have been handled earlier and so on.

Next, rearrange each of the main headings.

Your next task is to rearrange each of those sub-headings under each heading in a logical order, again to ensure that the flow of your article within each section is smooth and the article will move in one direction, instead of in many directions.

Let's look at an article entitled 'Twenty-five years ago'. It is a topic that is always current and one that never seems to disappear for very long, although the article itself was written several years ago. It is about changes that have occurred in the workplace during this period, and offers a possible solution. Such an article could look at several related topics within this subject area, such as the changes themselves, changes in education, unemployment, the future.

Using this example, let us look at the broad picture — your idea that you want to write about changes in employment over the past couple of decades or so. Read the article carefully. Consider different aspects of it to see how each part fits within the headings, how each paragraph links with that preceding it and the one following, and see how each section (under each heading) glides into the next section. The article has been marked with pointers. Consider each of these too, to see how such an article is composed.

You might, for the article 'Twenty-five years ago', have a series of headings such as this:

Introduction

What was it like years ago to get a job?

What is different now?

Education

What value was education then?

What value is a degree now?

How are graduates usually employed now?

Health

Is unemployment good for our health?

How is unemployment likely to affect health? Why?

What is our future with regard to work?

What's left without work?

What's it going to be like in years to come?

What's happening in the work scene?

New trends

The unemployment problem

Changes in public attitudes

Lack of humanness

Will all jobs disappear?

Probably not

Then what's a good alternative to work?

Now reconsider each of them. You may decide that some of these points could be better included in another article covering a different point of view. Delete them from the current list, and keep them for later.

Check that your major and sub-headings still remain in a logical order.

Twenty-five years go

By

Frederick Staffer

Twenty-five years ago it was quite easy for most people to find work of some type. A woman – young or old – could sit for a typing test, pass the test at thirty-five words a minute, and be offered a position in the Australian Public Service. Short-term and casual work was readily available. A person could usually find work fruit picking, as a 'garbo', working at a service station filling cars with petrol or giving vehicles their grease and oil change and their thousand mile service. Jobs were generally plentiful, turnover was high, and there were usually others to step into those newly created vacancies.

There have been changes. There is no longer a category of 'typist' in the Australian Public Service. Fruit picking is mostly carried out by mechanical harvesters. Petrol stations are self-service enterprises. Cars are serviced only by specially trained mechanics, and at ten-thousand kilometre intervals. Garbage bins are emptied by one operator driving the truck. *Note the change in shift in this line from the previous paragraph.*

Other industries too have seen dramatic changes, changes sometimes brought on by advances in technology, sometimes through drives by firms to achieve efficiencies in operations and as a means of lowering overhead costs. Broadcasting stations can now be operated efficiently by the use of computers with only three staff, including administration personnel. The publishing industry has been changed with the advent of computers so that whole categories of positions no longer exist. The newspaper industry has likewise changed.

Note how this is changing direction.

In an attempt to raise profits, many firms no longer have middle management positions.

These changes are not unique to Australia.

According to the ABC's Business Report, a huge international construction company with an annual turnover of over $30 billion per year has recently reduced its Swedish headquarters from a staff of 4000 to just 200 people. The Mercedes Benz Factory in Germany no longer has any middle management positions. And in Japan, according to Barry Jones in his book *Sleepers Wake*, the automobile factories are largely automated and each worker builds nearly 140 cars per year, whereas in Australia, mechanisation is lagging behind Japan. Consequently, car manufacturers are closing down in Australia, as they are in other countries too.

Now we can look at what is happening elsewhere in the world— but notice that still the theme flows naturally.

Education

Twenty-five years ago education usually assured a person of a good job. Year 10 was considered adequate for most positions. Then Year 12 was accepted as the basis of many jobs. A university degree guaranteed the holder of almost any reasonable position applied for.

Now we look at a shift in emphasis— education and how that has changed over the same time.

Today, two degrees will not guarantee a graduate any position. The best that someone with a PhD can expect is a temporary, part-time academic position. It was claimed last year (ABC's Law Report) that if all the law students studying law now were to find employment in that field, then every law firm in Australia would need to double in only four years. Clearly, this is not going to happen. And in science the prospects are even worse — some universities in England have already closed their science faculties.

Make some points controversial.

It is common for companies to receive over a thousand applications for many jobs they advertise — certainly, more than 500 applications for many positions is frequent. A mail order catalogue from a firm in Canberra in January said that its staff were well qualified to help the buyers — four staff who wrapped the parcels had degrees in law, science and the arts. This is typical of job prospects for many graduates. These few employed people will provide the taxes that run the country and pay the social security of those who don't work.

Or will they?

There would be considerable resentment from those who work and who are expected to provide services and social security to the rest of the country. There is already resentment towards those recipients. It will get stronger in any society.

The future for those who are not running the rest of the country is looking bleak. But need it be?

Health

Through media reports, we are being made aware of trends towards higher unemployment due to the rapid rate of change within the workplace. The physical environment — in this case, the workplace — is one of the principal factors affecting the state of our health.

Introduce other related topics — health is affected by being unemployed, so such a topic introduced here is appropriate.

Most dictionaries define health as a state of soundness of body and mind. Just how sound can we expect the minds and bodies of the future generations to be, given the rate of change within our physical environment?

If we continue to expect to be employed, we are in for a rude shock.

And perhaps this is what we will have — a whole lot of shocked minds trying to cope with the new reality of continual change. No such thing as job security any more.

Human beings need security. Over the past decades we have been leaning more and more towards money as our security blanket. And to have money, we need a job. No job — no money — no security.

Since the early 1970s, life expectancy has been extended to over eighty years for females and more than seventy-five years for males. And those figures are increasing with improvements in health care. These indicators reflect that the general level of health of Australians is better than it has ever been.

How can we hope to maintain this level of good health if we are entering an era where there will be fewer jobs; and those jobs that are available will be subject to constant change?

Our general health often depends on our state of mind. And if our minds are caught up in the notion that money — and a job — are security, then we are heading for a decline in the health of the general population. Studies have shown that chronic unemployment and under employment lead to poor housing, crowding, lack of privacy, broken families and a sense of helplessness — and an increase in ill health.

Perhaps our best defence against the constant change in our physical environment is to begin to change our way of thinking about that environment. Or will what we consider at this time to be 'alternative lifestyles' become the norm in the future?

The future of the individual

There are numerous sayings such as 'life is what you make of it ...' It is up to every person to make the most of what time and resources he or she has available.

In a controversial or thought-provoking article, lift the readers' mood by offering something positive, but don't let such a swing detract from the facts that you have written before.

A reduced working population means greater leisure time. It means more time for socialising. And it means more time to develop personal skills, such as hobbies, sports, and through these contacts, make friends. People who have skills should still be able to use them in the societies of the future. They should be able to make their craft items — pottery, wood carvings, dried flower arrangements, wrought iron, and pursue hobbies like welding, woodworking, growing vegetables. It is a chance for learning, to develop education and other skills — if there is a demand for them. But any skills help a person to develop fully, to use what talents they have, and to mature fully. A life without any activities would be seen by many as an empty life, one without purpose. But ... what will they pay for these activities with?

New trends

Further reductions in staff can be expected with changing behaviour, such as with shopping. Departmental stores are reducing staff, and making the customers serve themselves. Assistance in many retail centres is scarce. Many people choose to buy their goods online, such as books, where they can buy products for much less than if they go into a shop. Many large stores now have an online presence — Myers, David Jones, Dick Smith, Office Works, Harvey Norman.

The unemployment problem

During the election campaign for a Federal election some years ago, the Opposition at the time was claiming that it would reduce unemployment to zero, but refused to define what 'zero' unemployment really was.

The Australian Council of Social Services (ACOSS) estimates that in addition to those officially registered as unemployed, there are a further 25 percent categorised as 'hidden' unemployed. These are people who want to work but for whom there are no jobs. This means that the true unemployment figure is about 30 percent. Most of those families would have relied on two incomes, with 25 percent now relying on one income, ten percent relying only on Social Security benefits.

Changes in public attitudes
Many reports commissioned by governments and carried out by universities and social organisations all claim that unemployment will get worse, not better. Many such reports claim that jobs for youth, for example, will disappear within five years. This trend will then flow onto other age groups. Already older workers (that is, those over forty or forty-five years of age) are finding it almost impossible to find suitable work. Many of those are now over 50 years, so the problem for them is even harder now. *Introduce new aspects by means of headings.*

But despite this outcome, many people, perhaps having old-fashioned attitudes and ideas, still believe that there is work 'if you want it'. That sort of claim may have been valid thirty years ago!

But not all of those unemployed can buy a lawn mower and mow lawns, although lawn mower manufacturers would like this to happen. Nor can every one of those unemployed be able to serve in a bar — there are not enough bars, not enough customers. Public attitudes towards the unemployed will have to change. Often it does change (albeit slowly) in individuals when those people suddenly find their employment has disappeared.

Lack of humanness

Of those jobs available, many now are in computers and use modern technology. That in itself creates social problems. There has, for example, over recent years, been a trend towards contact activities, such as massages and contact sports merely to have some contact with other humans. Otherwise, the only contact with the world is through keyboards.

This trend will continue, as a considerable amount of work can be done over the Internet. The Internet and email systems can be used for contacting anyone in the world. There is no longer face-to-face contact with other people, no longer social discourse, normal conversation. Smart phones have made physical contact almost impossible. The people using this new technology are becoming more and more isolated and cut off from other people.

There will always be some jobs

It is reasonable to expect that some jobs will exist in the future — someone will be needed to build dams, to pour concrete for footings of factories and houses, and to run service stations and to repair broken water pipes and to ...

But not many people will be needed for these tasks as new equipment is invented, and as even newer technologies are introduced.

The barter system

One suggestion. The barter system has operated successfully for many centuries. It is a scheme where money is not exchanged, but goods and services are. Labour is exchanged for fruit or vegetables or for other services. Goods are exchanged for other goods. Properly managed, these schemes can be successful. There is one operating in the Blue Mountains west of Sydney. There, the basic unit is the 'echo' where one echo is worth a certain amount of time, or value.

Encourage your readers. Use short sentences occasionally to keep the pace fast and exciting.

And a society with little money will not necessarily be a poor society. For example seeds for vegetable are reasonable cheap. Twenty dollars will buy enough seeds to provide a family with fresh vegetables for about a year. And for many, gardening is a worthwhile pastime.

Add the names and contact details of suppliers at the end of the article for the benefit of your readers.

* * * * *

NOW YOU CAN BEGIN TO WRITE!

An outline is merely a plan. Arrange all the headings with sub-headings indented, in a logical, developing sequence. Headings are the themes of topics and carry much of the supporting detail. The outline also suggests a tentative paragraph structure.

Keep the heading under which you are writing on the computer screen. A few lines beneath the current text, type the next heading. Put in a page break after that heading, so that all subsequent headings are thrown over to the next page, out of the way. The idea is to concentrate on the paragraph or two you are writing, but to keep an eye on the next aspect of your article. Keep this next point in mind as you write, and the paragraphs will link naturally. Get into the habit of using linking or transitional phrases. Link a paragraph to what has immediately preceded it. Join paragraphs where possible by implying 'which leads me to say ...' Such linkings can occur at or near the beginning of a paragraph or at the end of the previous paragraph – the last sentence can introduce the next angle of the article. You can also link paragraphs by words showing logical relationships, such as 'therefore', 'however', 'even so'. Any transition should shift readers easily from one part to the next without jolting them.

As you tackle the next section, bring up the subsequent heading, but keep all other headings over on the next page out of sight.

At this stage, don't spend too long deciding whether a particular word is right. Use another word that means roughly what you want to say. Get your thoughts moving, and keep them flowing. Don't spend too long at this stage deciding whether a point of grammar is correct. The main thing now is to get the first draft down.

Rough out the full article, then gradually develop and refine it, keeping the total effect always in mind. We will look at reworking this draft under editing. But consider a few more points.

You have chosen your topic. The editor of a magazine wants you to write the article you proposed.

Before you even begin, ask yourself some questions:

Who am I writing this for? [Identify and consider the reader.]

Why am I writing this? [What is my purpose in writing this article]

Which angle is best for this magazine?

What do I want to say?
But first, consider some more points.

THE ART OF WRITING

Having chosen your topic, where do you get your words? From within! The words will come to you if you let them.

There are several ingredients of writing: purpose, strategy and style, and conventions – grammar, usage and mechanics. These aspects determine the limits of what you can do as a writer.

The most basic ingredient is purpose. The purpose of writing is to communicate. Written communication involves not only a writer but also a subject and a reader.

Subjects do not exist solely in themselves. They exist in the mind and in the words of the writer and, potentially, in the minds of the readers as well. As a writer, always think in terms of your readers.

How long should your article be? The writer's guidelines will indicate a preferred length for articles submitted; perhaps the article can be as long as necessary to 'tell the story'. This does not mean a long article with lots of padding.

How much information should be included for a particular magazine? Provide as much information in your article as is called for by a particular publication. Some magazines require little information, others want a lot of facts. The depth of your subject should fit the magazine, and the readers. On the other hand, a subject should not be trivial or simple-minded. Few articles discuss all there is to say about a subject. They treat only one aspect of the subject.

THE READERS

Respect your readers. Do not take your readers' interests for granted, or suppose they have endless patience to wade through difficult expression and wordiness. Your task is to make the readers' job as easy as possible. Good writers take the trouble to be clear so that their readers do not have unnecessary difficulties in understanding what is written.

Ask yourself about the readers. What do I expect from them? What do they believe and value? How can I affect them by what I say? What will offend them, therefore what must I avoid writing? What objections might they have about my ideas? Are they likely to understand irony and wit? Bear in mind that not all your friends will have the same interests, so do not expect to write to please everyone, or to interest everyone. You won't succeed if you try.

Always explain difficult ideas clearly. But of course you should never define the obvious.

CHOOSING A STYLE

Style is what you do with words, sentences and paragraphs. Style is a particular way of writing.

What particular style does the magazine adopt? For example, the old-fashioned style? Get into the habit when you write, to imagine that you are talking to someone in a relaxed, casual manner, trying to explain something. This keeps the writing personal and friendly. But remember that readers must understand you entirely by the words you have written, and your style must at the same time reflect the preferred style of the magazine

The writers guidelines may include a preferred basic style, but your style will develop in time, especially for a particular type of writing.

Correctness is not necessarily the essence of good writing. Effectiveness is often confused with correctness. Writing effectively requires more than correctness. Observing rules, such as grammar, does not in itself make prose good. Disregarding them seriously reduces the effectiveness of otherwise good writing.

Purpose, strategy and style are determined by you, the writer. You decide what you want to do, plan how you want to achieve it, select the words, and compose the sentences and the paragraphs. But these decisions must be made within the framework of rules, or conventions. The conventions fall within the categories of grammar, usage and mechanics. In written communication, we do not have the benefits of speech, such as tone of voice, inflection and gestures for emphasis.

Read the work of writers whose style you like, and try to discover what you like about each piece they have written. Is it the short sentences they use? The long sentences? Humour? Humour is sometimes useful as a means of improving an otherwise dull subject, but does the editor like humour?

POINT OF VIEW
Point of view relates to how a subject is presented: personal, such as first person (I, me, my etc) or impersonal. The subject and purpose should determine which point of view is chosen. The degree of formality may determine

choice. The point of view must be consistent throughout, but sensible.

TONE

Tone is the feeling of an article. It contains the writer's attitude towards the subject, and the reader. Tone can be serious, or one of amusement, or ironic or unemotional.

Tone is unavoidable. You imply it in the words you select and in how they are arranged. Phrases such as 'as we know', 'I think', 'I believe' help form a two-way communication between the writer and the reader.

SENTENCES

Flow between sentences should be smooth. For the writing to be coherent, every paragraph must satisfy several criteria:

- relevance: every idea must relate to the topic;
- effective order: ideas must be arranged in order of importance; and
- inclusiveness: nothing vital must be omitted.

PARAGRAPHS

Keep average paragraphs between 120–150 words. Below this, the paragraphs may be disjointed and need developing; above this, they may tire readers. Individual paragraphs can vary, of course, from one or two words upwards, but don't use too many very short sentences or paragraphs. Short emphatic sentences can carry conviction, which is essential in effective persuasion, and they suggest a speaking voice rather than a rigid tone. The readers will appreciate this.

AVOID ANNOUNCEMENTS
Avoid saying that you intend saying something, such as 'I want to make it clear'; 'let me tell you something'; 'let me say'. Because you are telling your readers something, you do not need to add these sentences.

UNDEVELOPED IDEAS
Sometimes writers include irrelevancies, such as side issues that are not part of the topic. A common mistake of new writers is to bring up ideas interesting in themselves but beside the point. Stick to the point you have chosen.

PUNCTUATION
Vary the punctuation for greater impact. Use short, crisp sentences for fast-moving pace, long and jointed sentences to slow down the pace.

Considering these points will help you focus on exactly what you want to write, for whom, and why.

Here are a few interesting points to consider.

Look at the difference between the statement '... the Murray River, the Colo River and the Mitchell River in Queensland', and '... the Murray River, the Colo River, and the Mitchell River in Queensland'. The difference the comma makes after the Colo River is to say that the location of the Colo River and the Murray River are not in Queensland, whereas in the first phrase, the sense is that all three rivers are located in Queensland.

Don't use phrases such as the Murray and the Darling Rivers. The correct names are the Murray River and the Darling River.

And consider too the difference between phrases such as 'headings should be left-aligned' and 'headings should be left aligned'. 'Still warm water' is different from 'still, warm water'. The first implies that the water was heated and remains warm; the second phrase implies that the water is warm but not moving.

Don't overuse 'one' and 'ones' as there are better words that are more accurate.

When using proper names or nouns, check the accuracy of the names. For example, compare the Melbourne Botanical Gardens, with the Canberra Botanic Gardens; Australian Chamber of Manufactures, not Manufacturers, Green Cape, not Cape Green, but there is Cape York and there is a Cape Melville. These terms are relevant to articles such as those on family camping.

OVER-WRITING

Plan on writing more than is needed so you have words you can cut out. This is easier than writing more material when you think you have finished. If your article will finish at 2,000 words, try writing about 2,300 to 2,500 and cutting it down to size. What do you do with the surplus that is cut out? If it is good, keep it for possible use in another article. It is surprising how often those little gems come in handy in providing a line or two for another article, or even giving a writer ideas about a possible topic for a future article.

TITLE

Consider a title that will appeal to the readers. It should catch the readers' eye, and make that person want to read on. The title should give you the theme of the article. It should clarify the subject, and arouse interest for your readers. The title, however, does not take the place of the opening paragraph. Titles should be both informative and eye-catching. After you have finished, be sure that the title continues to fit your theme or treatment of the subject.

CONCLUSION
The closing should be proportional to the length and complexity of the article. The closing should leave readers with something to think about. The paragraph should not be so hard as to say 'this is the end, and this is what you should understand.' Be more subtle than that!

ILLUSTRATIONS
Does a particular magazine want illustrations? Will photographs or drawings improve the chances of getting your article accepted? Good photographs will improve your chances of having an article accepted. Can you use a camera to take good photographs? Submit all photographs as JPEG images, and edit them if you can to enhance those parts that are most relevant to your article. If you can't use photographic software, don't worry. The production team at the magazine will fix that. This will enable the production team to crop to the area that should be included in the published copy of the magazine.

Can you do the necessary line drawings, or do you know someone who can? If you can provide them, you are fortunate. But do not pay too much to get someone else to illustrate your article, as you would be greatly reducing your profits.

If you illustrate an article, NEVER incorporate the illustrations into the pages of text. This is not only inconvenient to an editor, but the practice can cause a lot of difficulties in the page design. Indicate in the text to which illustration the particular sentence or paragraph refers by adding a comment in brackets at the end of the line [See drawing 3] and so on. Keep the illustrations, such as line drawings, one to a page only, clearly numbered, with the caption on a separate sheet of paper. When you number or label the drawings, make sure your reference is well clear of the drawing itself. Using a non-print pencil will be an asset to the magazine's technical people. The reason for all this is that often drawings, photographs or other illustrations are scanned and either enlarged or reduced to fit the allotted space, or cropped as needed. If your number on the illustration is too close, you will be causing someone else extra work.

THE ART OF EDITING

The art of editing can really be described as throwing away more than you keep, or as the art of rewriting to improve any written work.

Don't believe that every word you write is sacred, so be prepared to delete many surplus words for the sake of clarity. Begin by deleting all clichés, phrases and sentences that mean very little, and most adjectives and adverbs.

Deleting words is like working in an overgrown garden—the more weeds that are removed, the clearer become the gems that are left. With gardening, the gems can be rearranged to improve the overall aesthetics of the garden. So too with good editing.

Be ruthless in striking out what is not necessary. A large part of revision is chipping away excess words. Look for clarity. Strengthen important points by expressing them in short or unusual sentences.

Eliminate generalisations. Revise awkward repetitions of the same word, for example, 'such'. Replace vague abstracts with precise words having richer, more relevant phrases.

Remove all redundant words, such as really, actually, basically, physical location, really, do in fact, at this point in time. Make sure every sentence is worded correctly. Make sure every word is the right word. And don't make up words.

Be alert for errors in grammar and usage, and in spelling and typography. Make sure your punctuation is adequate and conventional but no more frequent than clarity or emphasis requires.

Beware of mannerisms of style, such as beginning too many words with 'but' and 'and'. Avoid writing long, complicated sentences. Without a draft, you have nothing to revise; but without revision, your draft remains shapeless and incoherent. Both are necessary for clear, effective writing.

In editing, you will get rid of what is redundant or irrelevant. The result should be a coherent whole. What follows is a long list of what you should eliminate from your article, or other points you should check.

HEADINGS

Check that the title of your article is relevant to the content, theme or treatment of your subject. Ask if all headings and sub-headings are relevant to that theme, and hence your title. If not, change your title or delete some of the headings, or better still, reuse them for another article on the same subject.

CLICHÉS

Clichés are dull and unoriginal. Examples of clichés include: at this point in time; on the back burner; level playing field; cool, calm and collected; history tells us; the bottom line. Don't use any of them.

COLLOQUIALISMS AND SLANG

A colloquialism is a word or expression appropriate in conversation. It is out of place in popular written work, for example we have a swell program; square (meaning old-fashioned); cool. Such expressions, however, are fine when you are writing for young people who talk like that. This comes back to what we mentioned earlier about considering your readers.

Don't use colloquialisms such as booted a goal, the satellite was rocketed into orbit.

WORDS TO USE

A good writer does not use words beyond the capacity of the readers. If you must use an unusual word, define it where appropriate; for example, in writing for mountaineers, the word crampon is alright to use. In a how-to magazine for different readers, this word would possibly be meaningless to a large portion of readers and would need defining. It is unnecessary to define any word that is, or should be, within the general knowledge of the readership. Ask yourself if a definition is necessary for your targeted readers; you should not ask your readers to consult a dictionary unnecessarily.

Check words that sound alike but are quite different, such as waste and waist, so telling a fisherman to tie a plastic bag around his waste would have a different meaning from telling the same fisherman to tie a plastic bag around his waist. Also, metre and meter — an engineer checks his 10 meters, while a child crawls 10 metres. But there are problems with some words if you are writing for American magazines, or British magazines. American spelling is meter, the British spelling is metre for the same object. Confused?

SIMPLE WORDS
Always use simple words instead of long, complicated ones; proceeded — went; demonstrated — showed; narrated — told.

HYPHENS
Don't hyphenate words in your copy, even if the word is too long to fit on one line of your page. The hyphen could be inadvertently reset and appear in the wrong place in the printed text. Better still, try using shorter words. Hyphens are acceptable, however, where there is a clear confusion. Compare recover and re-cover (as in a chair), recreation (a holiday) and re-creation (to create a second time).

EMPHASIS
Use italics instead of underlining words such as plant names, but don't overuse emphasis, such as italics,

underlining or bold. Such emphasis should be used sparingly. Bold is alright to use regarding a danger: **Always wear protective eye protection when grinding steel. The process will throw out red-hot sparks that could lodge in your eyes.**

REDUNDANCIES

Use only the word that means what you want to say. Every word, every sentence must be relevant. Not every word you write is sacred, so be prepared to cut heavily. Avoid phrases such as bisect [in half]; modern life [of today]; [vital] essentials; [sufficiently] satisfied; it is [clearly] evident; he hanged himself, [thereby taking his own life]. The phrase 'or something' is overused in speech, but means nothing at all (it is probably a shortened version of 'something like what I have said', or 'something similar to this'. This should never be used in writing.

Redundant words include outside of the city, also, front side, left side, right side, (but definitely not backside), walking on foot.

These are words that fill no function, convey no meaning and contribute in no significant way between reader and the writer. In other words, don't say in ten words what can be said adequately in three.

Use the minimum number of words possible; for example, words can be deleted from these examples: twenty metres [away] from the creek; we [ourselves] ...; our [own] ...; such as ... [for example] ...; look [out] for opportunities; the [biological] scientist; on the basis of (by); as a result of the fact that (because); the way in which (how); people who enter university to study for their degree ... (undergraduates); emerged victorious (won); had an effect on ... (affected); have to have a knowledge of ... (know); tends to be... (is); finally, [the last point] ...; so far as is [presently] known ...

The following statements were used in news bulletins. Look at how stupid such claims are! The prime minister toured the drought! He went to the earthquake! The houses moved closer to the flames! (Sorry, but these examples were taken from actual news bulletins.)

Check all spelling, particularly words that end with suffixes such as able/ible, en/ern.

JARGON
Jargon is technical language that is misused. Technical language is simply the highly specialised language of experts writing for other experts. It is acceptable and efficient. But beyond its proper use, it is limited.

OBVIOUS BY IMPLICATION
Now see what you can do with the article you have written. Rearrange your work after you have cut out all unnecessary words. Ask: can I amalgamate any paragraphs when I rearrange them? Can I then cut out more words? Delete until you cannot delete another word. Writing improves in direct proportion to the number of words eliminated but only up to that point where not another word can reasonably be cut.

When you have finished your article, use a cover sheet and send it with a simple covering letter to the editor. Decide whether you will post the article with all the attachments, including photographs and illustrations, or will email everything.

Some editors will return page proofs for checking. These are copies of the pages that will appear in the magazine. Don't go changing anything, unless something is very wrong. Just mark errors; the editor will decide whether or not anything warrants changing. It is very expensive to change text at this stage. The copy that you sent to the publisher should be your 'final'. Learn a lesson from this for next time, then look for another magazine you can write for!

REVIEW YOUR ARTICLE

Review your article and see how these points relate to what you have written.

- Is the title effective, appropriate and catchy?
- Does the article work?
- Is it long enough to get the message across?
- Is it too long?
- Are there any unnecessary words?
- Are there any clichés?
- Would it appeal to the intended audience?
- Would they find it interesting?
- Would they think about the message after they have read it?
- Would they learn something from it?
- Is there anything in it that is unnecessary?
- Is the flow smooth?
- Is the punctuation about right?
- Are the lengths of sentences about right?

- Are the lengths of paragraphs varied, and about right?
- Are the words too complicated?
- Does it have a smooth flow — introduction, middle and conclusion?

Use this questionnaire for each of your articles. It will help keep you on the right track!

COVERING LETTER

When you send off your article either by snail mail or by email, send a covering note to remind the editor that he or she was interested in your article.

"Thank you for your interest in my article entitled *The use of fodder trees for livestock production in Australia*.

I am pleased to enclose the completed article. Also enclosed are several photographs of trees that have been grown as a source of feed for livestock.

I look forward to seeing the article in print."

COVER SHEET

Your article should have a cover sheet, with your name and address, telephone number, the title of the article, the word count and the rights offered.

CHOOSE ANOTHER MARKET

Rework the article you have just sent off and, hopefully, had accepted, and submit it with a different slant to another magazine. Remember, both (or all versions, if you want to rework the same topic in different ways for a number of magazines) must be significantly different, aimed at different readers.

Earlier, you wrote down topics of interest and to each of those, you allocated several magazines that could be interested in your ideas.

The point here, then, is to choose the next magazine, send a query letter outlining your new point of view, and get an acceptance.

The benefits of reworking an article are there — you do not have to research a new topic. You do not have to start from scratch. You do not have to become familiar with a new subject just to write one more article.

Sometimes articles can be adapted to several magazines. Articles based on an original idea can be different, for different readers in each case.

You can also reuse your articles in other ways — using the first and second publishing rights, and overseas rights, as distinct from rewriting your article. Usually a magazine will stipulate what rights it must buy — first Australian serial rights, first New South Wales serial rights (this applies particularly to newspaper articles), and some require all rights, in which case the article should attract a much higher payment to reflect your reduced publishing opportunities. If you sell a magazine first Australian serial rights, you can then sell second Australian serial rights to another magazine that is willing to reprint published articles. This will usually attract a much smaller payment for the same work. If you sell first (and second) Australian serial rights, you can then sell first American serial rights to an American magazine; first New Zealand serial rights to a magazine there, and so on. This means that your writing can attract a far wider and diverse readership, with appropriate increases in payments. And again, once your article has been published in another country, second publishing rights apply there too.

NEWSLETTERS

In this age of digital media, it is just so easy to write and have articles published. What about developing your own newsletter? Software that will create great looking newsletters is available, and is easy to use.

Now that you know how to write articles for magazines (and, of course, newsletters), there is nothing to stop you from developing your own newsletters to distribute on-line, in a field that you find so interesting that you want to share with other readers. Here's your chance.

And instead of waiting up to a year for payment, you can attract almost immediate payment from sponsorship to your newsletter, or from paid advertisements from businesses with an interest in the subject of your newsletter.

Once you have built up a reasonably large database of subscribers, you can quote this number of readers to businesses when approaching them for sponsorship. You might as well use this new media for your own gain. Businesses no longer spend a fortune on radio and television advertising. They don't pay telecommunications companies thousands of dollars to list their business in the Yellow Pages (many of which are being made obsolete anyway). And newspapers are certainly feeling the decline in revenue from what was previously lucrative advertising.

They are turning to on-line publications, and why shouldn't they advertise in your on-line newsletter? After all, you now know how to write articles for newsletters and magazines.

Chapter 10 The How-To Article

As I mentioned in the introduction to this book, writing is all about sharing — you share ideas and information, and of course you encourage the readers to develop skills, perhaps skills they never realised they possessed. Get them to extend themselves with your encouragement and help.

The how-to article is really all about sharing. You have expertise in an area, and this is your way of sharing your knowledge with others who want to develop some skill.

The how-to article is, really, one of the simplest to write, yet many people find them the hardest.

Here's the clue.

Pick your topic that you want to write about. But that's obvious anyway.

Now imagine giving instructions to do something, such as cooking or doll-making, a cross-stitch project, a woodworking project or a welding item where the readers will want to use the skills you are about to teach them.

This type of article is best considered as a 'build this project with me' type, or 'let's work on this project together and I will show you how to get the best results'. If the readers feel they have a mentor there to help them with their project, they might develop more confidence. Since you have already made the item, and are showing them how to do the same, they will assume you are the best person to help them.

With the how-to article, it is often best to assume that your readers have at least the basic skills or they are wanting to learn a new craft. After all, it is not possible to teach them carpentry or cabinet making or welding if they have not even the basic knowledge of what tools they will need nor how they should use them.

But ... there is nothing wrong with an article, if a magazine is interested, in telling readers how to set up, say, a metalworking workshop.

In this type of article, that would become the first in a series of articles on welding. You would need to tell your readers what tools they would need to acquire so they can at least get started.

The readers would need to know the price they could expect to pay for the basic tools. You would need to give a range of prices starting with the basic tools. At the other end, you would need to give the brand name and the likely cost of the better quality tools for those who have always wanted to take up a new skill or learn a new hobby, and would be prepared to spend more money and get tools that are going to last them for many years.

If you have been commissioned by a magazine editor to write a series of articles on a particular subject, the next article in the series might be one on using the basic tools.

You would also need an article on using tools safely. You don't want to lose your readers because they have electrocuted themselves before they can move on to the first project.

If, however, you are writing for, say, a woodworking magazine that specialises in articles of the how-to nature, you definitely would not need the first two classes of articles — setting up a workshop, and using the tools safely. The readers would already have that knowledge and those important skills. The editor would not be interested in including the obvious to readers who are experienced. You need to give the editor, and thus your readers, at last something new, or some new way of doing something that is going to make their time more productive.

There are, really, two types of how-to articles — one for those with the necessary skills to carry out your project without too much difficulty, and those who want to learn from scratch and develop those skills to a reasonable level.

You will not be talking to tradespeople. They would not be the people who would be interested in your article.

So pick the level of readers you could reasonably expect to read and appreciate your article — either the reader with sufficient skills who just wants to know how to do something, or the reader who wants to learn the basic skills from the ground up.

Now pick the most un-handyperson you can think of. Imagine him or her in front of yourself as you write, and write it for that person.

The most un-handyperson could be a friend who really would like to make something but does not have the skills to go about doing a competent job.

This is not an instruction to talk down to your readers, or to put them down. That person you have identified could be intelligent and hardworking, but with skills in an entirely different area to those you are good at.

This is where you can share your knowledge.

Often this type of article is greatly improved with the use of clear diagrams — put this piece of wood here, so you can do that ... One diagram would show the layout of the pieces of material you are talking about.

You will need to build up the project. You will need a materials list — details of all the materials they will need before they can construct the cabinet, for example. Give them the cut lengths — they don't want to be told to buy eighteen metres of 4 x 2 timber. They would prefer to know they will need six pieces each two metres long, four at twelve hundred millimetres long, and so on.

You will also need to give them a list of other hardware — hinges, welding electrodes, plugs, solder, flux and stains, and all other components. Many people go to the hardware store to buy everything on one visit.

Advice about the best types of material — such as types of timber for that particular application, or software for their computer for their scrap booking project, is essential. They won't get very far following your advice if they don't have the right materials or the right gadgetry to get them started. They simply will not be able to follow your instructions, and you will have failed them.

Now take the reader through each step slowly, assuming at least a basic level of competence. Every amateur will want to take their time and feel their way through the manufacture of the item you are helping them with.

At the end of the project, they will want to know how to finish it off so they can take pride in their recent accomplishment. What is the best varnish to use on their new cabinet? What is the best way to treat their new trellis they have just finished welding so it won't rust? And what is the best type of paper to print out their scrapbook project, or for their baby album? If you don't tell them they might use the wrong finish or product, the project will not meet their expectations, and again you will have failed in your job as teacher.

Your readers will want to know exactly how they can use the item they have just accomplished. If it's a baby photographic album, suggest the number of copies to have bound. Suggest one for the parents, one for the grandparents, one each for aunties and cousins — everyone who might be interested in seeing the photographs. Some people — in fact often many people — do not think of all recipients of such items. A reminder will help them. They don't have to include everyone on your suggested distribution list.

Similarly, if you are taking readers through the process of welding a wine rack, suggest how they could enhance it — perhaps by putting it in a conspicuous spot in the family room where their visitors can admire it. Suggest a couple of bottles of wine that you might even include in your own wine rack, to give them an idea of how they could best utilise such an item they have just made.

And similarly with woodworking projects, suggest the best location in their house or apartment that would suit their new bookcase.

THE HOW-TO BOOK

This is where this type of article gets interesting. What is the difference between a how-to article, and a how-to book? The difference is that the article is about one project, the book comprises many such articles. Each chapter of the how-to book would contain only one project the readers can make for themselves.

In such a book, it would be okay to assume that your readers have bought the book to start with, having not many developed skills, merely an interest in starting something new. Give them the encouragement and the confidence to develop their new hobby.

So such a book, if it was about welding or carpentry or scrap booking or developing books of holidays or baby photographic collections, would have instructions they could follow so they can buy the right materials or the right paper, and the correct tools, with an article on their safe use if you will be instructing them to use hand tools, to one on safety in the workshop, to safe work practices.

With safety, make sure you tell readers about the risks of the materials they will be working with. If you are encouraging them to use timbers such as treated pine, many of the red woods, cedars and perhaps other common and popular types of timbers, you must warn them about the dangers of breathing in the fine dust from sawing or sanding such materials. Or if you are giving instructions on welding, you must warn them to work in a safe environment — keeping the work area free of clutter, free of cords they are likely to trip over, the risks of carrying steel (yes, it is heavy, and I think if gets even heavier as those carrying it grow older). You must warn them about the hazards of breathing in the welding fumes. And you must warn them to wear protective ear protection at all times they are operating machinery. And of course, they will need to be reminded to use adequate eye protection if they are drilling or grinding steel — even the best twist drill bits can shatter and spray sharp pieces of hardened metal into eyes.

I mentioned how-to books. If this interests you, rather than trying to get individual articles published, then see the chapter on self-publishing. That's the way the literary world is going, so follow the how-to instructions given in that chapter and take your own how-to projects to new levels in the twenty-first Century.

Chapter 11 The Travel Article

Do you enjoy travelling around the world, to exotic destinations, or to well-known and loved cities? Or do you like to explore in your own backyard — along the scenic coast perhaps, or waterfalls in a particular national park?

Travel writing opens up many possibilities for writing. It gives the writer an excuse to travel, even if it is only in his or her mind as the writer recollects memories from their most recent trip.

Writing travel articles is in some ways similar to writing any other articles, including researching your topic well, deciding on a style, writing for particular readers.

With travel writing, your readers will want to know about new places, new adventures in their favourite cities, or new areas they could be tempted to travel to for their next vacation.

But here is the trap. It's a big trap.

Nearly every destination in the world has been written into the grave. Call up any catalogue of books and you will get an idea of how extensively travel writing has already been covered.

There are hundreds of books about what to do and how to do it and where to go in Paris. Publications about New York, London, Sydney, the main capitals of the world, have had their contents exhaustively spread around the world in publications — books, magazines, on the Internet, brochures, and television programs covering travel.

Where does that leave you, the writer?

Think creatively, think about what is left. And think of all the aspects of a city or a destination that would interest you if you were to travel to your favourite destination just one more time. You have seen all there is to see in Paris, for example, so what's left to write about there?

Surprisingly, there's still lots to write about that is not generally covered by other travel writers, and is not covered in the popular media.

Take Paris again (sorry, but I am rather partial to Paris). There are many quiet places in Paris, despite the city attracting thirteen million visitors each year, combined with its normal population of around fourteen million people.

Even in a city of that size, there are quiet little spots. There are quiet laneways with their unique architecture. There are cobblestone streets that are never included in other travel writings. Don't you think your readers will be interested in something different?

I often claim that when I travel, I don't look at things. I experience them. Other travellers have similar ideas.

Paris is the home to many famous writers. Their houses are often marked with a plaque, such as that of Orsen Wells in the quaint arty-crafty area of Saint Germain de Près just up from the Seine. Victor Hugo's house in Place de Vouges is open to the public. Visitors can see where this great French writer wrote his plays and his poetry and other literature. His tomb is in the Pantheon — a great and historic building in Paris. Victor Hugo shares the Pantheon in Paris with many other famous French people, including other writers from the past — Voltaire, Dumas, Zola.

How many people have been on a literary trail in Paris? Paris has hosted many writers past and present (France has more writers who have won the Nobel Prize for literature than any other country).

You have Chateaubriand who was one of the great writers of France who launched the Romantic era of literature. He spent time in Paris too. But he grew up in the town of Combourg in Brittany, but spent time at Saint Malo and Dinan in the north of Brittany.

Wouldn't a literary trail including one or two writers be interesting? Apply the same theme to writers of London, New York and anywhere else you would like to travel.

Do you like to get away from the business of the huge cities from time to time? Where do you escape to at times like those? Are there quiet little boulevards you have enjoyed? Don't you think other travellers would appreciate advice about visiting such areas?

In the town of Jerilderie in New South Wales, there is an interesting trail associated with Ned Kelly's gang of bushrangers. Jerilderie is the only town in New South Wales the Kelly gang ventured into and caused their usual havoc. There is a bushrangers trail around the town, with plaques marking sixteen buildings of interest. There's the newspaper office where Ned and his crew gave the editor a letter outlining their grievances against the government and against their treatment (they did have a bit to whinge about, because they felt they were harshly persecuted). The letter was published, but one hundred years later. The court house there has a story to tell, as does the blacksmith's workshop. Ned's gang stole the police horses, took them to the blacksmith to have them fitted with new shoes, and then charged the bill to the police.

Have you heard of Jerilderie? Have you travelled to Jerilderie? Possibly not, but a day or two in the town makes for interesting exploration. Visitors can learn about a couple of days in the lives of this notorious but famous gang.

But whatever you wish to write about, much of it will already have been covered by writers before you.

So how do you get that brilliant article about your ideal travel destination accepted for publication, and hopefully, receive a generous payment for your efforts?

Start by studying the magazine you wish to submit to. What does it look like? Is it a low-cost production, printed on cheap paper? Is it glossy with lots of advertisements? It is the advertisements that generally pay for the magazine to be produced, so if the magazine gets a lot of revenue from advertising, the editor might have some money left over to pay you for your contribution. But check rates for payment—they might be included in that panel on page three showing who does what at the magazine—the editor, production staff, advertising agent and so on. There might be writers guidelines telling you what they want, how they want it presented, and anything else they will require from you, including maps and photographs.

You can always obtain the writers guidelines from the magazine. They should be available from the publisher's website. If not, send them an email and ask for them. The guidelines will tell you about the magazine's current requirements. This information will include preferred length in number of words, the preferred style, and much more. They should include deadlines for submission. If they do, make sure you meet those deadlines with plenty of time to spare, especially if the magazine is featuring one destination, and you want to write about that destination.

You have decided you want to write an article about a holiday destination of your choice, and have chosen the magazine that looks hopeful. Then send the editor a query letter. In it, outline the article you want to contribute, your experience in that location, your experience as a writer, other publications that have published your work (it's like applying for a job—you have far greater chance of getting a job if you already have one). So too with contributing. Editors prefer to work with writers who have already been published. If other editors think their work is okay to publish, then we'll go by that, will be their attitude.

Writing travel articles is rather different from writing, say, the how-to article, or the descriptive article that you would write for popular magazines.

Travellers are happy people (at least they are until they pass through airport terminals, get lost overseas with their passport stolen and left with no money). They want bright, newsy information pieces straight from someone who is full of enthusiasm, who knows his destination, and can transfer that enthusiasm through his writing. Because they are generally a happy bunch of people, you can write the article with humour—after all, lots of travellers have amusing experiences to tell their family and friends on their return home. Write about some of those less serious happenings. They are what makes travel memorable. Even some of the things that make you feel miserable at the time can, on reflection, prove to be rather amusing and memorable incidents.

Shakespeare wrote about the comedy of errors. Can you write another comedy of errors?

So write with enthusiasm as if this is the most important thing you will have done all year. You enjoyed the place, so write it to encourage others to go to your destination as well.

You will write the article with commitment—this is where you must go, and I'll tell you why! That should be your attitude.

You will research your article well, but you will write it from a personal experience, with a personal point of view. Don't make it weak—I went to New York and had wonderful time. That just won't work, and won't get past the editor. Expect the article back in the mail next week.

Travel is about colourful experiences—the culture of exotic destinations, the costumes, the music, the restaurants. So fill your article with colour, and make it vivid, with lots of interesting descriptions, must-see scenes, and interesting people to meet.

If your article inspires others to travel to your destination, they will want to know all about the place. How do they get there? What transport is available? How do they travel around when they are there? What can they eat? What's the standard of restaurants? Are there places you would not recommend? Why would you not recommend them? How much money would they need to take with them for the duration of their stay there? How long would they need to stay in a place to see it properly? You should include information about accommodation in the region. Perhaps if you enjoyed your lodgings while on vacation, and were prepared to recommend those places to others, this might be very useful, and will mean that the person booking a trip won't need to spend too much time looking for other places to stay. But the reader will want some choice — don't give them only the name and contact details of where you stayed, but don't swamp them with too many alternatives.

Because nearly all travel destinations, and aspects of travel have been covered before you even thought you would like to become a travel writer, you will need to have a fresh approach, or point of view, for your article. You can be creative. You must be creative! Make sure you cover some out of the ordinary aspects of your destination. You must make the article interesting. It's not just the use of one thousand words that's going to be a workable article. It's going to be the use of colour, humour, descriptions that are concise and accurate. Evoke strong feeling in your readers to make them want to follow your adventures so that they too will want to share the experience.

The personal approach is usually best for this type of writing. Anything else becomes just another narrative, and your readers won't be looking for just another narrative. What did you do? Why? What parts of the trip fell apart for you? Did you put them back together? How? Did you need help to do so? Was help readily available? Are the bus shelters comfortable when you get to a city late at night and find that everything has closed for the weekend, all restaurant staff have gone home, and that one takeaway unfortunately burned down last weekend. That in itself sounds rather fun, so tell your readers how hilarious that experience was. But on the other hand, the place you experienced on your recent travels might have been rather scary. Tell why you found it to be so. If they like scary incidents, they might be interested. If they don't want to scare themselves silly, it would be a place they would want to avoid.

What are adventurous things travellers could attempt? Have you even cycled around the Arc de Triomph in Paris and survived? You have? And you survived without needing more than a month's hospital treatment? Then you must include that. What trips are there out of town — perhaps day excursions, or interesting villages just beyond the city limits? Why were they so different from the city you came to see? Tell them.

Can you speak Venusian? What's that? Good question, so provide your readers with the answer. Did you have problems with the language? Can't read labels? That makes interesting meals. Being unable to translate the contents of cans and containers, my meals have sometimes been a mixture of dried egg power mixed with baked beans and topped off with a green sauce (I am not sure what was in the green sauce, but it tasted okay, and gave me enough energy to see the city delights the next day). Think of some of the concoctions you have created though your inability to translate foods in tins.

Make your travel destination — and hopefully theirs

too — rather exotic. Give them something to think about in your destination that could be experienced only in that one location. Have you ever had the taxi ride from Hell, where the driver didn't understand speed limits (I don't think it would make much difference anyhow), drove mostly on two wheels, screeched to a sudden stop and then admitted he had no change when he saw your fifty Euro note? Tell others what to expect. The taxi industry might not appreciate your free publicity, but your readers might.

Can you take photographs to illustrate your article? Of course you can! Digital cameras have made taking quality photographs foolproof (well, almost. There is still a lot of room for improvement for those home photographers who neglect to allow the camera time to focus itself, and all their pictures are blurred). So as you take each photograph, look in the screen and make sure that it looks fine. If not, take another one, and another one — until you get it right.

There might still be some cropping and editing to do on the photographs when you get home. The good news is that nowadays there is some excellent, reasonably priced photo editing software that can straighten sloping horizons, make a dark picture lighter, and make a light picture darker. And if you got that lamp post on the edge (or a white van that seems to come into almost every photograph you take in the cities of Europe), and you decide the picture would be much better without that hair of another tourist blowing into view just after you pressed the shutter, then you can improve it to a certain degree. But if at the time you think the picture you have just taken would not be suitable for any publication, then take another one. Take several. Take fifty of the same thing.

Photographs taken with digital cameras don't cost you anything until you print them out, so you are not out of pocket by taking numerous photographs of the same scene. You will have lots to choose from. Try taking pictures from slightly different angles, showing some interesting architecture or a monument in the background, or another road with its traffic snarls.

Good quality photographs should at least double your chance of acceptance of your article. Similar quality photographs should at least double your payment. But don't count on either of these eventuating. Some magazines prefer to send their own photographer out to take the photographs they want. And payment might be slow. So book your next trip away only after you have received payments from several articles you have had published. You might have lots of time in which to research your next trip!

Chapter 12 Writing For the Web

Wow! I can hear you saying. What's so creative about writing for the web? Why should I be interested in that?

This is, as you already know, the twenty-first Century. Everything is on the web, or the Internet. Every business is there, or if they are not there, then they effectively don't even exist in the modern era.

Every individual who is doing something useful — filling a gap in the world, creating something, or who wants to be found, is there, or should be there, or, again, if they are not there, they don't even exist.

Writing for the web is not boring, because it is as creative as any other field of writing you can think of. You can make it interesting. You can make the text worth reading.

And you can write text for other individuals, and other businesses, who are not able to write effective text for their own websites.

And that is what makes this field of writing so interesting.

Although the Internet is a fairly recent innovation, during the first ten years of that time it was slow to become effective. It was only when individuals and creative people and businesses saw the potential in this new form of promotion and publicity that the web even began to become of any real importance. New search engines such as Google pushed it along merrily. And it hasn't stopped.

Other forms of media have slowly ground to a halt. Newspapers are losing their appeal and popularity for advertisers. Television is losing revenue. Television channels that only a decade ago were bringing in billions of dollars in advertising revenue each year are struggling to even make ends meet. In fact, many television channels are not even able to keep above the bottom line. And that's the way the world is going.

So how can I interest you in becoming a web writer? I could do that by telling you that writing for the web is different from writing an article for a newspaper or for a magazine.

Web writing is not all about writing lots of words. It is writing precisely, because web users — that is, people who read the text on websites, want facts. They don't want to have their time wasted on anything other than what they are searching for. They don't read text in detail. They skim, or scan. They pick out the parts of the page that are important to them. They want succinct text providing all the details right there that they can access on their smart phones and tablets, often while they are on the train, the bus, or waiting for a meeting to start. And many of them access information during those meetings too if the meeting proves to be rather boring. They want to make their time productive, and anything that prevents them from achieving that goal is a waste of their time.

As a potential web writer you must know how to get the web pages for which you write text on the first page or two of the modern search engines.

A website can consist of as many pages as is necessary to get the message across to web users. This might include product descriptions. It might include the service individuals offer. It might include information about the area they service. As a tradesperson, location could be important because a plumber will not travel thousands of kilometres to repair a pipe. But a web writer could consider the whole world as his or her domain. And there is nothing to stop clients contacting writers from around the world if they think those individuals can provide the service they are looking for.

When you do work on the web, your little town in the bottom end of a country has no boundaries.

Many writers develop effective websites not only to promote themselves, but to promote the services they offer to clients. Clients here could include businesses from around the world, those organising sporting events, or organisations, motels and other accommodation providers in desirable holiday destinations. The range of topics for web writers is limited by a writer's imagination. And being creative people to begin with, they have a good head start.

So let's start and write the text for your own website.

The home page (the entry page that web users will come to when they find your website on the search engine listings) will contain basic information about you, what you do, what you can do to help them. Remember that it is important to tell them what you can do for them, not how good you are in your own business. You are providing them with a service, so you have to tell them about the service you will provide to them.

The home page is a summary, and won't go into any depth.

The second page would contain more detailed information about you as a writer, from the point of view of how your experience is able to help the readers achieve what they want. Although it is tempting to write about yourself and praise up yourself, the purpose at this stage is not that!

Page three could list some (or all) of your publications, and other work experience as it relates to writing, and also to the kind of business you are in. If you are a good writer, and you are a keen sports person, then it is important to tell readers this because people will see how your love of sport and your enthusiasm for the same games or activity can help get their message across. In other words, you know what you are talking about.

You will need a contact page. This could contain the area of the world you are located in, or country. Don't give your home address. There are too many people who have other ideas about personal information. They will dial a telephone number to see who is on the other end of the line. A mobile number is ideal for this, as anyone with less that ethical reasons in mind won't be able to steal your identity — a real concern with so many people these days, and with very good reasons. You will need an email address.

Now comes the fun page if you want to boast about your skills. It's the 'About Us' page, where you can tell readers all about you, your background, how you got into writing, what you have accomplished in life, any awards you have won, the types of work you have been engaged in, and anything else you would like them to know about you. So have fun!

Gone are the days where a static website worked wonders and constantly brought in business. Nowadays, search engines want updated information—material that will be updated every three or four weeks. Search engines will realise that the site is still active and that there really is a person at the other end of it called Me—Writer.

You will have noticed that blogs are becoming a part of just about every website these days. And there is a very good reason for this. If you have a website that tells readers everything you want to convey, then blog entries will maintain that site in a fresh and interesting way.

Blogs (or web logs) can comprise anything you think is relevant to your readers (not necessarily to yourself), that contains information that is worth reading. Readers will turn to those blog entries you upload on a regular basis, and get updated information. And the search engines in turn will respect you because your site appears to be live and should be truly worthy of indexing. The more entries, the higher the site goes in their results. That's the theory of it, at least. Other criteria come into play too. Links to social media such as Facebook, Twitter, links to other important sites that receive numerous hits and visitors every month will all play a part. If you can get your site linked on several popular sites, you should notice, at least over time, that you appear further and further up towards the top of the search engine results. But all that can take time.

A blog is a running page of your thoughts and ideas.

This page can be updated with whatever frequency you wish, but to be most effective, aim for updates at least once a month. Try twice a month until you start to run out of things to say.

The content of a blog page is just as important as the content of the rest of the website, and just as important as your book itself. Don't underestimate the value of a blog page.

A blog entry should have content that is worth reading. It should have content that the readers want. It should add to the value to your book or your website by adding additional information, perhaps instructions for a new woodworking project, or a new recipe for a pavlova you have just made could be valid entries. But it must be information of quality, and saying something readers want to read, or about something they want to learn. Don't just put on it a series of family ramblings. And don't fall for the trap of friends and family members, usually in good faith and good will, writing a blog and then you find it doesn't say much at all. If it isn't worth reading, people won't read it. But if you update the blogs frequently with quality information, then they will come back to your website.

By having regularly updated blogs, this paints you as an expert in your field. If readers find they can rely on the information in your blog, then they will come back to your site because they can trust you. And if they come back to your site often enough, then they are more likely to buy your book. And isn't that what you want?

A blog entry should never be blatant advertising, not even to promote your own book. People want content, and information, so provide them with this. Occasionally, though, it is considered reasonable to put at the end of some entries (perhaps no more than one in every five blog entries) that more information can be obtained from your book and include the URL where they can find your book details. Include that URL even if it is attached to your website. It is far easier to just click on a hyperlink and go to the page than it is to scroll to the top of the page, look for the page containing the information about the book and then take action from there. They probably won't.

So how long should a blog entry be? There's no set length, because the page can expand to any reasonable length. But don't make the page too long otherwise readers will get bored with it and won't finish reading, and so they will miss out on learning all about your ideas.

The subject of a blog should be relevant to the subject of your website, but this rule is not set in stone. You could have quotes from famous people and a detailed interpretation of that quote, or a piece about that writer. But try to tie it in with the subject of the website to keep it all along the same lines.

One warning here is needed. You will (that I can guarantee) receive a lot of emails from dubious websites that want to exchange links with you – if you include their site on your website, they will include yours on theirs. Ignore them unless the webmaster of the site approaching you is in exactly the same business as you. Search engines will realise there is no connection with these dubious sites, and will push your site right to the bottom, or, worse still, push you out of existence altogether because they realise what is going on. So if you get asked to exchange links, delete the email and move on.

So how do you go about setting yourself up as a web writer? Appreciate that writing for the web is an art, and is a specialised field of writing, like few other fields of writing. Realise too that not everyone can write the text for their own website. This is where you come into the picture if you are good at it.

You promote yourself as a web writer, specialising in writing text for small business websites and corporations, perhaps. Large companies will have their own media team who specialise in writing corporate reports, press releases, and could easily accommodate writing the text for a website. Tell readers what you can offer. The success you have had in getting other clients' sites listed with the major search engines should carry a lot of weight too.

The listing in search engine results is important. Some businesses can invest several thousands of dollars in developing a website. If the search engines do not value the site, then the site will be listed way, way down in the results, and people will not be able to find it. So the businesses that have spent twenty thousand dollars building a website have effectively wasted every cent of that money on something that is useless because it won't drive traffic to them.

Search engine optimisation is the key to having the search engines list websites high on their results. If you can get your site on page one, or better still as the first entry on page one, you are doing very well. Boast about it. Tell the world about this achievement! It is worth blowing your trumpet for this fame. You are competing with maybe eighty million pages all providing a similar service, so if you can displace all those and get in the results ahead of them, it will make them jealous.

This is how you do it!

Headings are important to the text and the document, and they are important to the search engines. Search engines use headings to determine content, and thus position in their search results. Where possible, insert level 1 headings, and plenty of level 2 headings. But don't overdo it!

Search engines go on content. Decide what people will be searching for when they call up the page containing the text you are writing and then work backwards. Without making it obvious — and this is important, incorporate around four percent of those key words or phrases you have identified in your text. Get around the obvious overloading in creative ways. Don't just repeat a phrase to get that four percent of content. Disguise it more subtly than that. If you have identified a keyword as 'text', then say something like 'We can create text for small businesses. We write text for organisations. The artistic community enjoys the text we write.'

If you go to a page and look for 'source' (it might be something sightly different on different browsers), you will see headings that include key words, page content, page description, page title. These are written into the background of web pages as meta tags. The information in the meta tags is crucial for search engines to find the web site. So make sure you include them.

The title you give to each page should reflect in no more than a few words what that page is about. Each page should have a different title so search engines realise that each page on your website is different. If two pages were effectively the same, try amalgamating those two pages and then editing the content heavily to reduce redundancies.

The 'content' will include a short paragraph telling readers (and more importantly, the search engines) what that page contains. So it must be realistic, and the words on that page description must also be included in the text of the page itself. The words will be matched, and if you do not have the same words in the text as you have in the content description, then search engines may push that page right to the bottom, because they will suspect something a little less ethical than they would like to see.

Keywords used to be important, but so many webmasters abused the system and search engines no longer rely on them for page placement. But you can include them if you want to.

When you write the text for your website, or for someone else's website, you will get differing opinions about how long each page should be.

One thought is that people want brief descriptions, where they can go straight to the information they are looking for. The other way of thinking about length is that search engines are entirely word dependent. If you have a lot of words, with the key words repeated in a creative way, search engines are more likely to rank your page higher because it will be exactly what people are searching for on the Internet.

The answer lies somewhere between those two lengths.

If you are developing your own website (and you will save a fortune if you do), you will have to submit that URL (the actual unique web address) of the website to the major search engines for indexing, otherwise they will not know that it is even available.

To do this, you can do the indexing process manually by going to the search engine, scrolling through until you find a mention about adding a site. That, unfortunately, can take several weeks to several months before the page appears on the results, because these days search engines want to know that a website is going to stay on the web for at least a reasonable time. So by delaying the indexing for several months, then it has passed the first test of its longevity.

The alternative way that is much faster is if you have one website, or a friend who is prepared to help you, you can add a link to the second website from the first. When search engines go through one to detect updates or changes, they will find the link to the second one and go through that and add that to their index.

Update your website as often as you can to keep the content fresh, keep the site simple and easy to navigate, and user friendly. And if you can, or if you can get a web designer to upload your site for mobile phones and tablets (they use a different format, one that is shorter and smaller), that will be a benefit to those who no longer use a conventional computer. And that number of people using smart phones is increasing exponentially each year. This will ensure your site is compatible with the modern devices, therefore they will be more user friendly.

One way in which you can promote your new book, or the book of short stories you are proud of, is to let readers get a taste of what the book is about. They won't be able to feel the book, turn it over, to assess it, but you can help them to assess it by giving them a sample of its contents. I like to include the contents page, Introduction, and the first chapter. They will be able to asses the whole book with this much information. The content page will be important (unless your book is a novel) because they will be able to see what is beyond that first chapter. They will assess a bit of the book, and realise the rest of it must be just as good as what they have already read.

Put this material in PDF format, with a link on the relevant page of your website. Learn how to insert hyperlinks in the text and make sure the hyperlink is the correct one. You can check this by clicking on all the links, including page links, when your website goes live on the Internet. Then make sure you check the link to the sample chapter you are offering your readers. On all websites you work on, make sure they contain no broken links. 404 Error page — unable to find the page message is a most frustrating message to receive.

Chapter 13 Writing Your Book

You have come a long way since you started reading this book! You are now almost ready to write your own book.

I know, you look at a blank computer screen, shriek, then call up the Internet and start surfing your favourite topics there. It's not very productive if your intention was to write a book.

Let me make it simple for you. Hopefully in the process you will be able to remove that dread of nearly all writers — writers block. This is like the stage fright actors often encounter. But with writing, the task ahead of you is just so enormous, that you don't begin.

How long have you wanted to write that book? A year? More than that? Quite possibly.

Let's say that you enjoyed that short story that you wrote. You liked it a lot, it was full of your emotions, and said exactly what you wanted it to say. Even your mother gave you an unbiased opinion of it, and her praise got you motivated.

If you have a number of short stories, and you think they are all good, then perhaps you should consider publishing them in a book as a collection of your short stories. One short story was good. Two short stories are better, and three make the first two even better. Before long you have a reasonable number that you feel would fill the pages of a book. And how many short stories comprise 'a number' of such stories? That depends on you. A book of short stories that fill between one hundred pages up to say one hundred and fifty pages would be a good number. So if your intended published book will run to one hundred and fifty pages, and each short story is only ten pages long (around three thousand words), that would be only fifteen such stories. And that would be a nice size for a collection of short stories that would inspire any reader to read what you have written.

Do you remember that how-to article we discussed? A collection of how-to articles would be suitable for publication in a book, provided they are all on a similar theme.

If your hobby is metalwork, or welding, your how-to articles could be the basis of a book 'How to ...' You would apply a logical progression of articles in such a book — start off with an article (or a chapter) Getting Started. This would motivate the reader. The next logical chapter, or article, would be a discussion of the tools they will need. The next one would follow on from this one — Using the tools safely. This would be followed by the chapter Safe welding around the home. And then you can go into the articles or chapters — one chapter or article per project.

Readers will want a book that is worth their money buying and their time reading. They want instructions, and they want it so they can follow the instructions. So try to write each article, or chapter, with a 'build this with me' attitude. They will need to be taken through every stage, otherwise they wouldn't be buying your book because they would know everything they needed to know.

But what if your book is not a collection of short stories, or how-to articles?

The next way to overcome that dreaded writers block applies whether your book is a novel or a more serious non-fiction work. Both can be treated the same, and the result makes the whole writing process so much easier. This is to break it down, and break it down some more, and then break it down even more.

Consider this.

BUILDING YOUR MANUSCRIPT

It's about time we considered the art of writing your book—that is, putting the words down on paper, or most likely on your computer or tablet.

The first sentence is usually the hardest sentence of all to write. If you find yourself sitting and staring at a blank page or an empty screen for minutes on end with nothing happening, don't give up. Just ... write something. Get a sentence, any sentence, down on paper or on the screen. Follow this with another sentence. If these first sentences seem like rubbish, you can always discard them later. Often just the act of getting your first ideas down on paper will help other thoughts to flow. Edit them later—discard the junk but for now ... just begin.

Something that often prevents the first words from coming is the intimidating thought of the sheer volume of words that have to be written. For instance, a typical manuscript might require around 60,000 words to perhaps 100,000 words, which amounts to about two hundred to three hundred pages of typescript. Do you believe yourself capable of writing this much material? Probably not, and your page will remain blank for a long, long time if you approach the task at hand in its entirety. The enormity of a task is often enough to detract any would-be author, builder, sculptor or scriptwriter from even beginning a project.

Your manuscript will not be written all at once, but word by word, paragraph by paragraph, or page by page. Try to build up your story like a house—brick by brick, from the bottom up.

With a book requiring 60,000 words or more, don't think in terms of the finished piece, but in terms of the size of the units or bricks with which you feel most comfortable. This might mean a page, half a page, or a paragraph.

These small units, added one to the other, will soon become a full-length manuscript—a few paragraphs, or a couple of hundred words a day will, in only a matter of weeks, add up to the 60,000 words you have to write. How long have you thought about starting that book you feel so strongly about? A year? More than that?

Seeing yourself making progress with your work as each 'unit' is written, can make the difference between the struggle and the triumph. If you get stuck with one section, don't stop, but work on another section that you feel more confident about. You will be in a better position to smooth any bumps and cracks when the larger part of the structure is in place.

Let's consider the hypothetical task of writing a book about, say, juvenile delinquency, and suppose our own basic writing unit is two pages—that is, we know we can write two pages (or about five hundred or six hundred words) about almost anything. Our job is to break down the 60,000 words required into manageable writing units of two pages.

The first step is a rough division that will form the main segments of your book. Let's say twelve segments, each one about five thousand words, or twelve pages, long.

The first segment should outline your topic and define your terms. This in itself may seem intimidating, yet, broken down further, that first segment of the manuscript becomes more manageable.

What is delinquency? My definition may possibly be different from yours, and different again from a social worker's ... or, indeed, from that of a high-court judge. So, perhaps ten definitions, each of several paragraphs (adjusted to suit the manuscript, of course) will take care of a major part of a chapter of your book.

WRITING YOUR MANUSCRIPT

Chapter Two might consist of around twelve pages devoted to the types of minors who commit acts of delinquency. Difficult, but again, broken down into units, we may get ten different groups of people who become involved in anti-social behaviour—discuss these groups on the twelve pages allocated, or a little over one page for each group. That's not too difficult, is it?

Chapter Three might look at the socio-economic factors of known offenders (a couple of pages), educational background (a couple of pages), the psychological profiles of delinquents (two pages), the background to some specific case histories, and family factors (each of a page or two).

Subsequent segments might look at cross-cultural differences: how is delinquency viewed in North America, in Australia or the islands of the Pacific?

Planning your manuscript at this stage will help ensure there is no obvious bias dedicated to a few segments, and almost nothing in the major issues of the subject. The manuscript will be smooth and will flow well.

Dividing a manuscript into small writing units that you can concentrate on, one at a time, will also help to prevent it becoming boring, with plenty of action, description, ideas and opinions on every page. You will be able to create a story that will leave the reader unaware that you, the writer, struggled and sweated over each and every paragraph.

We all get annoyed with people who repeat themselves in conversation. So when you write a book, limit the amount of repetition. Often it is necessary to repeat a point, albeit in a slightly different way, just to make sure that your readers grasp what has been said, or to reinforce a point. With practice, you will soon develop an instinct for what needs to be repeated, and what's best not repeated. And, indeed, what's best left unsaid. Don't repeat whole paragraphs just to pad out a manuscript so that it will fill the pages allocated.

If you are writing an article or a book or your new novel, employ the same technique of breaking the writing task down into small units before you begin to write. In a novel, something should happen on every page: different incidents to involve your characters in, different people in different settings, different historical eras. Breaking down the task will help you keep the writing fresh and fast-paced.

It's your house you're building ... use 'bricks' that you can handle comfortably. Don't strain yourself handling bricks manufactured for someone else with capabilities that would outstrip even the most accomplished builder ... or writer.

LENGTH

How long should your manuscript be? It's not so much a matter of how many pages, but more importantly how many pages are needed to get your points across.

As a rough guide, the average page will hold around three hundred words in New Times Roman font, 12 point. So if you have two pages to make your point, you'd better write about six hundred words.

If you are planning on writing a novel with one hundred and twenty to one hundred and fifty thousand words, break down the whole work into manageable portions. Once you have done that, see if you can break down each section, or component of your book, even more. The more you break down those one hundred and fifty thousand words, the easier the result with be for you psychologically. So if you can, break down your one hundred and fifty thousand words into small segments that total one hundred and fifty thousand — try and you will be surprised at what you can achieve. Start by breaking down the proposed work into as many chapters as you think would be appropriate to what you have in mind. You can always amalgamate some of the shorter chapters towards the end if you need to.

Now you don't have to write one hundred and fifty thousand words. You have to write only one thousand words, about one hundred and fifty different pieces of action in your story. And nearly anyone can write one thousand words. That's only three or four pages on your computer screen, or about one and a half pages on your tablet.

If you write only one of those segments each day, your book will be finished (at least to first draft stage) in less than half a year. How long have you been promising yourself that you will write that best seller? I am sure you have been hoping to start it for more than six months.

Sometimes the sheer enormity of any task is enough to make many of us look for all the excuses we can so we don't have to start. After all, if we do manage to write the first thousand words, beginning at the beginning, then that leaves only one hundred and forty-nine thousand words left. You haven't even made a dent in the manuscript yet. It's at this stage that most writers call it a day and look for something more rewarding to do with their time.

None of those segments you have identified needs to be written in a logical order. Write the chapters, or the sections of chapters in the order in which you feel most comfortable.

Chapter by chapter, bit by bit, paragraph by paragraph, word by word, your book is built up using bricks. If you don't like carrying huge bricks, then use small bricks. Use pebbles if you need to—no one will ever know how you managed to write such a large volume unless you tell them, and I am sure you wouldn't want to do that.

Break down that book of how-to ideas into as many components as you can. You might be working on one chapter, or one article. Don't write the whole article, or chapter, at once. Break it down. And then break it down even further. Use headings, and lots of them. Use sub-headings, and lots of them too.

Working backwards, your book starts off with the idea —your idea for your book. Then you break it down into chapters. Then you break those chapters down into segments using headings. And then you break even those segments down further using sub-headings. In the end you won't be writing two thousand words for each chapter, you might be writing no more than one or two hundred words about lots of different things.

You will then bring the novel together—all one hundred and fifty pieces of it—in the final editing. Clean it up, edit some more, and then re-write those parts you need to rework.

Your book must sound brilliant. Don't accept it from yourself unless it does. So keep tidying it up until you can't improve another word. It will become a process similar to polishing stone. The stone will be rough. You polish that a bit, and it becomes smoother and shinier. Polish it still more, and it will start to shine.

So too with your own book. When—and only when— your manuscript shines with brilliance (literary brilliance, that is) should you be happy with it.

PUT IT ASIDE

Most writers are the same. If they read what they have just written, they will not be able to read it through someone else's eyes. They will read what they think they wrote, not what they actually wrote. You can re-read it over and over, you can put it aside for a week, and try again, and you won't pick up those little things that are going to detract from your readers' positive experience.

You must leave it for several months after you think you have finished with the first draft. Only after a reasonable time, like three months, would you be able to read it afresh.

Better still, get someone else who has had some editing or proofreading experience and is good at their job, to check it over carefully for you. They will be able to pick up things that you will wonder how you could have missed. It's easy to realise just how you managed to miss so many stupid things — mistakes, and using the wrong word such as waste instead of waist. All writers do it, so don't feel awful when someone picks up on lots of little things. You won't be alone.

Never be content with producing sloppy work. Your first book should be your pride and joy — something you can hold up and look at, and show to others, saying 'this is what I wrote'.

Do you want to go on after you have gained your sanity again and write another book? Of course you will. But you will only want to write the second book if you are completely satisfied with the first one.

But having said that, you should try to make the next book even better. I realise the first book you write is the best you could get it. Does that really mean there is no room for improvement in the second book, and then in the third book? Even if you try to squeeze an extra two or three percent improvement out of the subsequent books, those following on from that first heroic effort will be even better. Now that's something worth striving to achieve, isn't it?

Chapter 14 Writing For Community Radio

What about entertaining listeners on radio? Now that's a real challenge. Community radio – radio for the people, by the people ... You have heard the rest of that statement. But community radio can be fun, it can be entertaining, and, through your involvement in community radio, you will be able to enrich the lives of many of your listeners. This chapter is not about producing or presenting specific programs on radio. This chapter concentrates on writing for radio. Many more aspects of radio, such as presenting, legal aspects, timing, are covered in my book *You're On Air*.

All radio programs need a script (try putting a program on air without a script and you will soon realise what I mean). Radio is not just one type of program, put together by one type of person. Because community radio really is for the people, by the people, then this certainly includes you, and your input and valuable contribution. Radio is communicating – communicating ourselves, our own personalities, to other people – this time not to our readers, but to our listeners.

In community radio, there are scripts that need to be written for everyday announcements. There is the news broadcast at least once a day. Writing a five- or ten-minute news bulletin every day is challenging. Especially when you have to ensure that your script runs to exactly ten minutes, not a moment longer, not twenty seconds shorter than the ten minutes allocated to it.

What about radio documentaries? Now that's an area of radio that demands special skills. You would need to select a topic that is interesting to your audience. You would need to present the material in a manner that is going to hold your audience's attention for the full twenty-five minutes. How demanding is that? How challenging could that be?

And of course there are radio dramas. Unfortunately not many dramas are heard on radio these days, because they require a lot of time to write them, to produce them, and then to allocate the air time in which they can be broadcast.

But why not, if you have that passion for radio dramas, write a radio drama for your community radio and have it produced in a professional manner by those who want to revive something that is far from dead? People, especially older listeners, still love the old radio dramas they enjoyed when they were growing up. This is one form of media they can relate to. So the radio drama audience is not dead—listeners are just not being given the material they want to hear. Through sharing, your radio documentary or radio drama could be played on numerous other community radio station across the country, and possibly beyond.

I have carried on a little about community radio. Why? That's because community radio has so much potential for new writers, and writers who want to branch out into radio. Some might see their career in radio. Community radio is the one means of getting into radio, doing the training necessary to master all the techniques of radio writing and radio production and developing confidence, and then offering yourself to commercial or public broadcasters. Community radio is a huge stepping stone on the path some writers want to follow, in the hope they can get into this exciting form of media.

Some see radio as dead. It's not. Television took over from radio in the early 1950s to 1960s in most countries, leaving radio far behind. It might be seen as the poor cousin to television, but look at what's happened to television in the past couple of years. Even that form of entertainment has dropped significantly in popularity. And after one hundred years, radio is still there. And it is expanding. We had broadcasts in the AM band at first, then it was realised that broadcasts made in the FM band gave a much better quality of sound (and radio is all about the use of sound). Now we are experimenting with digital broadcast technology that takes broadcasting to new levels of clarity and listening quality.

Age is no restriction. Many people become involved with community radio after their retirement, others contribute to radio while they are still attending school.

Most commercial stations, and state-run broadcasters do not present the range of programs they did in the 1950s and the 1960s. But community radio can fill that gap. While most programs on community radio stations are music programs, the aim of this chapter is to show that there is much, much more to radio than being just another disc jockey.

What's radio all about then? It's about entertaining people. It's about educating them. It's about amusing them. It's a process of enriching the lives of others.

Community radio is a process or an activity whereby you can become involved in a great form of media, of entertainment, and at the same time expand your writing skills to suit a form of media you might not have previously thought possible. Well, it is possible.

If you enjoy the arts, if you enjoy entertaining, if you enjoy helping other people learn something new, then radio could be what you are looking for.

The great thing about being involved with community radio is that you can expand your own talents, your own writing skills. If you want to write about the environment, about politics, about the economy, what the world should be doing, about ... well, they are your ideas, so this is your chance to expand on what you know and make the information you have available to anyone else. But that's what writing is about, isn't it?

Unlike commercial radio, community radio doesn't have sponsors telling the station what it can and what it cannot broadcast. While the station — any community radio — does have sponsors, that sponsorship must not influence program content. In Australia, there are laws that prohibit that sort of interference. The same rules might apply in other countries also, so you can be political, but still view your opinions. But there are limits on what you can say. You cannot criticise groups, individuals, people because of their race, sexual preference, lifestyle. But that's just common courtesy anyway, isn't it?

Community radio, because of its more or less freedom from outside constraints such as sponsors (or advertisers who dictate more than they should in the real world), you can offer programs of a more diverse range than you would expect from a larger, commercial radio station.

This means you can include literary programs, poetry readings, documentaries, radio drama, discussions about books, and even book readings. When did you last hear those programs on commercial radio? No, I don't remember either.

Whatever you decide to specialise in on community radio, you must learn the art of writing for radio. Writing for radio does have its own rules, and it does have other constraints, such as strict timing of the length of the program, and the time it goes to air. Breach those constraints, your program will sound sloppy, and that's not what you want to achieve. Aim for the best you can, aim for professionalism.

Writing good material for radio means getting away from the old idea that every thought, every phrase you ever thought of is important. It might be, especially to you, but if it doesn't fit the program, then it has no place on air in that particular program.

Prepare to sacrifice those words and phrases you once considered gems. Deleting words, often lots of them, will tidy up the end result and leave you with material that is worth saying, and worth listening to.

How do you go about writing for radio?

First, you don't want to sound too formal. Round off your phrases to make it more conversational. You'll abbreviate words, so those who'll listen to you ... Do you see what I mean? That sounds more friendly than if you told your listeners 'you will ...' Or 'who will listen to you ...'

Write your script so it sounds as if you are saying your words, not reading them.

Why do you even need a script? I admit there are some excellent radio presenters who do very well with conversational-type programs and they don't need a script. But they get paid a lot of money each pay day because of their skills. That's why the radio stations employ them. You might be one of the fortunate people who can speak fluently, coherently, and make sense without the aid of a script. That's good. For the rest of us, a script keeps us on track, reminds us exactly what we want to say, and in what order that material should be said, and how. There's nothing worse while you listen to radio than hearing someone talking a whole lot of words, but saying nothing meaningful. If you get tongue-tied, look at your script, and there's your very next phrase. Most listeners might not even pick up that you had forgotten your thought. Let them remain ignorant! And if you can't think of anything else to say? You can't even stammer the next word? Can't even think of the words you need? The result is silence. In radio, it's called the 'pregnant pause'.

With the choice of words, you have to evoke images for your listeners. Create pictures for your audience, so they can stimulate their imaginations. This is achieved by using only the right word, not just any old word. Every adjective should fit the noun perfectly, every phrase should be the one you want to use. Don't use a lot of words to fill up the minutes. Time like that is better used by playing music, or putting on a station promotional clip, or even a message from your sponsor.

Even with a good script in front of you, you can get caught by embarrassing moments. Like the sports commentator who told the audience that a cyclist was lucky because he had wind ... He had to correct himself and tell his listeners that the cyclist had a wind behind him and that's what gave him the lead. But ... Oops! Too late. If he had read through his script before turning on the microphone, that might not have happened. But most people have a sense of humour, so his slip might have been appreciated by lots of listeners.

Your audience does not have the benefit of being able to read what he or she missed. If they try to decipher what you just said, then they will probably miss the next three or four sentences, and then they will lose more than that. And you will probably have lost a listener.

How many listeners will you have, anyway? Although broadcasting goes live to thousands of people, and can be heard nowadays right around the world via the Internet, you should count on having only one listener — the person whom you should be writing for. It might be that person listening to you while driving their car, or waiting in the doctor's surgery for two hours. They are individuals, alone with their thoughts, so you will write, and talk, to one person. In other words, write your material for an individual, but lots and lots of individuals. This is what makes radio so personal. You are not broadcasting to the masses. Only to that one person.

Your first sentence would open the central theme of the program, tell your listener what that program will be about. Your second sentence should carry on from that one thought, the third sentence ...

Punctuation is also important. If you tell someone 'C'mon, Grandpa, lets eat, Grandma ...' everyone will know exactly what you mean. Leave out that one comma, and look at the result ... 'C'mon Grandpa, let's eat Grandma ...' Wow! Now we have cannibals in our midst.

So with the right words, the right sentences, and the right punctuation, you have to convey that information to your listener. So sound sincere. Have you even listened to a politician who sounded as if he didn't believe what he was telling you? Did he sound enthusiastic? Convincing? I am sure he didn't. And if he didn't sound convincing, why would you have bothered to have listened to him? You probably wouldn't. The switch on a radio is easy to turn to the OFF position. You don't even need to find the remote control.

How long should your script be? It's not the number of pages, but the number of words you will need to write. The average speaking rate is between 150 to 180 words a minute. So if you base your script on someone speaking at 150 words a minute and they talk at a rate of 180 words a minute, you will soon find yourself without enough material to fill your program. And a similar embarrassment applies if you aim at a fast speaking rate but a slower reader reads the text. Too much material, not enough time. Oops! That's bad radio. It is important to time yourself if you intend presenting your own material (the ideal situation), or get your intended reader to read it aloud, and make sure you make the necessary adjustments to suit their speed of reading. I once worked with a person who wanted to read a script of mine — a fifteen minute documentary on soils. He would send me an email — I am one minute too short. So I would add a sentence or two. Too long! So a few words would come out. But I could only take out the words that I could dispense with for the occasion, it wasn't a matter of cutting off the last two sentences. To get the right length, it might involve a few readings, out aloud.

Dates can sometimes be a problem. The New Year starts on January the first, not on January 1, which is the way you would possibly write it. The financial year ends on June the thirtieth, not on June 30. To make it easier, write out the dates exactly as you intent saying them.

If you become interested in working in community radio, there are some areas that will appeal to you more than others. If you are particularly artistic and creative, then there's radio documentaries.

COMMUNITY NEWS
But first, compiling the local news service will give you lots of experience in writing for radio. So what's community radio news about, then? Most, if not all, community radio stations will not have the resources to gather much beyond their listeners' boundaries, so let's concentrate on local issues.

This is where community radio comes into its own realm. Even commercial stations that are part of a network seldom cover news at a small regional scale. To national or

State audiences, regional material just would not have the same appeal, unless something dramatic happened. In smaller regional centres, seldom does something really calamitous happen.

A community radio could broadcast news that is relevant to its main interest. For example, if the station's main theme right across all or most of its programs were to be about the arts, then news about the arts would be popular. If the news service comes ahead of a science, or environment program, then news that concentrates on scientific news, or on environmental issues, would prove popular.

What's news? Some would say that it is any information about recent events or situations, and information, considered suitable for reporting , information that might not be previously known. This means, news should never be stale.

If you report news, or compile a news bulletin, keep the length to the station's allocated time for news — usually five minutes. Within that time, make each item reported on around twenty seconds. This means you will need fifteen items in your news bulletin, each of around sixty words. That's reading at the rate of around 180 words a minute. You will need 900 words for just this short broadcast time. Then at the beginning as a lead-in, you will have a brief announcement, '...this news broadcast is brought to you by our sponsors, Mickey and Felix Plastering.' And at the end, just a brief announcement reminding your listeners that the news broadcast was brought to them by Mickey and Felix.

In a local news broadcast, there is nothing wrong with grouping several items together, such as several controversial council development applications received by your local council, or different strikes that will affect transport in your region.

Once you have compiled your news bulletin, read through it, time it, and make sure it comes to the allocated time. No more. No less. Include in that the local time ... 'It's now ten o'clock, and that's news time.'

With community radio, you can be bold, creative and audacious. Try writing a radio documentary.

THE RADIO DOCUMENTARY

A radio documentary is more that a mere presentation of facts. Yes, you will be presenting facts, and hopefully lots of them. But the treatment will be quite deep, not just a glancing blow at the real issues of a topic. Get right into the depths of the subject. Since you are going to delve deeply into the topic, make sure you have a real interest in the subject, otherwise the program will be rather flat.

Local issues are important to local communities. State issues, or national issues could demand a lot of research, a lot of time interviewing the right people by telephone, and getting the right balance of views. Not always easy in large countries like Australia where you might be four thousand kilometres from the action you are reporting on. So with this in mind, keep the topic local.

Radio documentaries can cover so many issues. You can consider life histories, perhaps of a business man, or a retired radio presenter who worked for the national broadcaster for fifty years. You could look at life through the lens of a retired television cameraman, or a television news presenter. Then of course there are social issues, health issues, education issues, lack of business opportunities in small towns, land degradation in your local State forests. How good is your imagination?

Never force your preconceived ideas on your audience. It won't work. Your listeners will want unbiased information so they can make up their own minds about particular issues that probably do affect them. Who knows — you might even start a revolution. Or more likely, start a cause that others can become involved in and pursue that to get satisfactory results. It might be a subject the listeners hadn't even considered. If they get only your negative side of the story, that might turn them right off getting involved in anything.

A good radio documentary should never be low on content or substance, facts or issues. It must be presented in a way that is intelligible to your audience, easily understood, and easily appreciated. Not everyone will agree with you, but that's alright. They shouldn't have to. Make them think, but that does not mean that you should make them think just the way you do. If they all agree with you, how are you going to continue the debate, to get them to ask questions?

A good documentary will depend on a lot of research, and that's often what makes the compilation of a radio documentary so interesting to produce. You get to sift through the historic archives, the old newspapers, council records, and much more.

Leave your listeners with something to think about once your program has ended. End the program with a statement from one of the controversial interviewees who had something to say. Leave your listeners wondering if he had got it right. If you don't entice your listeners to continue their thinking about it, then it merely becomes entertainment for half an hour. You will want to aim higher than that.

A radio documentary should run to around twenty-five minutes allowing time for station sponsor announcements, and a brief introduction about the documentary — what it's about, who produced it. At the end, there will be time for another station sponsorship promotion, a summary of the documentary, the time, and a brief announcement about what you have lined up for your listeners next week.

RADIO DRAMA

If you are feeling really, really creative, imaginative, and all the other positive adjectives associated with creativity, think about writing a radio drama for production on your local community radio station. It won't be easy, but that's what makes this a rather worthwhile aspect of community radio.

Radio drama had its success up until the 1950s or 1960s when television more or less took over from radio. One gained popularity, the other lost popularity. But that does not mean that radio drama is dead. It's far from dead. Many people, especially older listeners who grew up with dramas on their radio, would still listen to a well written, well-produced drama today if they were aired. But unfortunate, they aren't. Possibly because of the time involved in writing one, the time involved in producing one, and finding the right actors to fill the parts puts people off creating dramas for radio.

If, however you have the time, the station has the resources, and you have enough enthusiastic friends who can act their parts, then you have the makings of a very entertaining program.

Like all radio work, you must stimulate the listeners' imagination. You will build up pictures through not only words, but sound effects as well, so the listeners can visualise the actions they are hearing. Sound can tell a listener so much. A cash register, particularly the old-fashioned ones, can tell you the people are in a shop, they have just made a purchase, they are about to leave the shop. Put some dialogue around that one sound, and you have something else again. The bell of the register gives the setting. Let the listeners imagine the whole setting.

The ringing of a door bell will tell listeners the play, or the scene, is set in a house, there must be someone home, and that another character is about to come into the story. Build up a simple scene with a sound, the sound of footsteps, perhaps a shuffling on the verandah outside, and there you have the makings of a story. This time, a story written for radio.

With the words, with the sound effects — the bells and whistles, the sound of the surf, bird cries, you can create all sorts of places for your listeners.

Add the cheering of a few people, and you immediately arouse their excitement — what are the people cheering for? Gee, there must be hundreds of people out there. Why do they want to come in all at once? The tension mounts.

You can, with the right sound effects, the right words, take your listeners to a tropical island, a parched desert, or a tropical rainforest, or to the beach. Add the buzzing of a few mosquitoes, and then you have included an unpleasant aspect into your story. If only real travel were that easy.

Many actors, producers and writers can express themselves through drama. Indeed, some psychological therapy is based on drama, where the participants of the healing group play out different roles. They report successful outcomes. The same applies to actors and writers who work on radio dramas.

The actors (and of course the writers) can express their attitudes to life, their beliefs, the emotions and feelings through role-playing. Anger can be released by acting in a socially acceptable way. It is alright for an actor to thump the table to make a point in a play. This might not be quite so well received in the domestic setting. Radio provides a constructive outlet for emotions.

With any acting, it's not what is said that is important, but the way it is said. The tone of voice tells the full story.

Radio drama has two important ingredients — characters and conflict. Take away one, the other falls flat. Conflict arises from almost everything we do, such as going on holidays. Conflict can arise from all those doing the packing, each wanting to take something the others don't want to see while away. One might insist that the television set goes all the way to China. The other refuses to go if the television set goes. Combine that argument with the right words, said in the right tone, and there is your conflict played out before you. But conflict is personal. We all react to different situations differently. Some might become bitter and angry when their boss tells them they are no longer required. This is the conflict from one point of view. I was once told that my contract was being cut short (the place of work had no money to pay me). My reaction was one of sheer joy—I hated the job so much I was going to terminate the contract anyway. People react to different situations in their own way. Not everyone is the same. Thank goodness!

It is possible to make a seemingly boring set of circumstances boil over with human interest, just by introducing appropriate conflict, and human interest. If your circumstances don't have much interest, and you are half way through your script, introduce a twist. A plot twist takes the whole play in a new direction that can breath new life into it.

You have a lot of volunteers who would be good at acting in your play. How many do you actually want to use? Sound effects can give your listeners a sensation that they are listening to thousands of screaming mobs outside the office. In reality in your play, keep the number of actual people small—perhaps no more than five or six. More than that, it is very difficult to remember who is who, and what they are and how they are related to one another.

All people are different. Some are deadly boring, and they do boring things at work, and on weekends. Some are the life of the office, always laughing and joking, and getting themselves and everyone else at work into trouble. I like people like that. Some are strong, others are weak. Some are domineering, others are downtrodden. Some don't take nonsense from anyone, others fall into line to keep the peace of the workplace. So when you write your radio drama, you will invent people to fit the role you have created for them. Make up people who will do everything you want them to do. To get this part right, spend some time studying people. Study them very well. Watch their general mannerisms, how they stand, how they talk, how they use hand gestures when they are engaged in a discussion or in an argument. Because there are so many different types of people, there are so many opportunities to put the right people together, with the wrong motive (conflict) to produce a radio play with the right amount of humour, tension, conflict, quarrels, and everything else you want your characters to get up to. Let your imagination run wild. After all, it is your drama you are creating.

I think one word of caution is essential here. Writing your radio drama script is one thing. Producing it is okay. But for the best effects, try to get professional actors to read the parts. These can be retired actors who are associated with your radio station, or someone in the community who would be able to get the right mood, the right feelings, across to your listeners. Proper acting can make the difference between an amateurish attempt, one that you might not want anyone to copy, and one that makes listeners ask for more of them. Aim for professionalism. You won't regret it.

Here is a short radio drama to give you an idea of how the dialogue flows. It also has minimal directions for the actors—a professional actor would know how to emphasise anger, and their emotions. They would know how to react to what is said to them, and that is an important consideration to remember when you write dialogue, not only for your stories, but particularly for radio drama. One person says something. The second person doesn't merely say a few words in response. The second person reacts to what is said. And with that reaction, comes across their emotions, and inner feelings. If person one irritates her, then she should be able to react with anger not only in her words, but in her expressions. The same applies if someone says something nice. The person responding will not only use nice phrases, but also their tone will be mellow, their voice kind and friendly. They should come across as nice people, merely because someone has said something nice to them. How do you react to people who annoy you?

Here's the sample script.

The Developer

A play for radio

CHARACTERS

Susan: A young woman, well educated, late twenties, with a serious personality.

Alice: A woman in her early thirties, with a care-free attitude.

Max Larsen: A developer, late-thirties, well educated and speaks with a slight accent.

SFX: INTERIOR OF A ROOM. CLASSICAL MUSIC PLAYING
SOFTLY IN THE BACKGROUND: HOLD. A GENTLE KNOCK ON
A DOOR.

SUE: Yes?

SFX: DOOR OPENS, THEN CLOSES.

ALICE: It's only me. Wouldn't you like the door open? This
          heat is stifling.

SUE: I thought you'd be making too much noise.

ALICE: [humorously] You should know me better than that. I'm
          as quiet as could be these days. Anyway, I've brought
          you some coffee.

SUE: Thanks. I'll clear a space for it.

SFX: PAPERS BEING REARRANGED.

ALICE: I don't know how you'll tolerate the quietness. I mean,
          after spending the past few years in the city, you'll go
          crazy.

SUE   Perhaps, but I'm rather looking forward to at least a few
          months of relative silence, and some time to myself.
          [CUPS RATTLING] As far as I'm concerned, I've spent
          long enough in the city, and long enough studying.

ALICE: You should have studied art, like I did. It's such an easy
          course. [A BOOK IS OPENED, PAGES ARE TURNED
          QUICKLY, THEN SLAMMED SHUT AGAIN]
          Environmental science. You can have that on your own.
          Anyway, what do you propose doing, now that you've
          returned home?

SUE: Home? Oh, here, you mean. This will do until I have
           time — and money — to look around for something a
           bit more elaborate. A place without the paper peeling
           off the walls would be great! I don't know how you've
           managed to survive in these cramped quarters. It's
           claustrophobic!

ALICE: [pausing] Nothing much has changed since you were
           last home. The population of the town has increased by
           seventeen, and the population on the coast, by one
           hundred and sixty-one.

SUE: I'll be happy if nothing much ever changes.

ALICE: But who knows? Who knows what will happen, and
           what surprises await you? From now on the place could
           become full of surprises for you. But I'm afraid in the
           next few days, the population of this town will decrease
           by one.

SUE: Who's planning on leaving? [pause] Not you!

ALICE: You guessed it.

SUE: You can't leave! I've only just returned, and here you
           are, running off already. I've hardly had time to say two
           words to you.

ALICE: That's because you've been cooped up in this little
           bedroom, gazing out at the mountains or at the inlet.
           Anyway, I'll only be gone a few weeks.

SUE: A few weeks? And who is he this time?

ALICE: Frank.

SUE: Frank? I don't recall a Frank in your life.

ALICE: Perhaps not. Anyway, he's been given an assignment with some magazine or other, to do a series of photo articles, on some place in South America. Lots of travel, that sort of thing. And I'll be doing some of the photography for him. At least, that's the intention.

SUE: Sounds great!

ALICE: And what are your plans? Are there any job prospects for you around here?

SUE: I think something should come up soon. If not here, then nearby. I don't really want to go too far away any more.

ALICE: Did you get mixed up with any of the political groups?

SUE: I wasn't at all interested in politics.

ALICE: You might be. [NEWSPAPER BEING THROWN DOWN] By the way, here's the newspaper. The good news is that your return made page forty-seven, and the other news …

SUE: [laughing] Page forty-seven!

ALICE: But the real news, that's on page one.

SUE: That's where it usually is.

ALICE: [cheerfully] It's about a development.

SFX: NEWSPAPER BEING TORN AND PAGES TURNED OVER.

SUE: Let me read that. [pausing] It can't be.

ALICE: It's good, if you ask me. It'll bring lots of people to the area. You might find that tall, dark and …

SUE: [angrily] I'm not interested in men! I'm only … That's the park … the reserve!

ALICE: So? You've got to expect development sooner or later.

SUE: [in disbelief] No one can build that monstrosity in the park.

ALICE: It looks like Mr Larsen is going to.

SUE: [angrily] He can't! It's public land.

ALICE: *Was* public land. Max Larsen bought the land recently.

SUE: I've always regarded that as my land … our land … the people's land.

ALICE: That's a rather selfish attitude to take, Sue. Anyway, I believe the story behind that sale was that our Council sold off a lot of their land.

SUE: It's not their land to sell.

ALICE: I'm rather happy about it.

SUE: How could you be? You grew up on that land. You used to go for walks with me after school. Mum and Dad used to take us there for picnics. Don't you remember?

ALICE: Of course I remember. But some things do change. Surely they taught you that at university? Development does happen. People do get ideas to do different things … Just because you want to stagnate around here, it doesn't mean that the rest of the world must stagnate with you.

SUE: Not wanting to see this outrageous sort of development take place in the park is not stagnation! [NEWSPAPER BEING SNATCHED AND THROWN ONTO A TABLE] Who is this Larsen, anyway?

ALICE: He's very handsome. You ought to meet him. He might be your type.

SUE: My type! Of what? Of bulldozer? Of demolition expert? Of ... of ...

ALICE: Don't get so worked up. [laughing] He once had a crush on you.

SUE: Well, he didn't make an impression on me. I would have remembered if he had.

ALICE: He was the local taxi driver back in those days, and you laughed because he wanted to take you home from the dance in his cab, and you wouldn't go with him. And he joked with you, saying that if you couldn't trust the local taxi driver, then who could you trust?

SUE: I still can't trust the local taxi driver.

ALICE: He's not a taxi driver any more. That was a few years ago.

SUE: I can't believe this!

ALICE: Don't start that again. Progress is what this town needs. That's the theme the Council's been preaching for a long time now.

SUE: I don't care what theme the Council's been preaching. What's the local taxi driver doing with all that land anyway?

ALICE: As I told you, but you were too busy sulking, he's not the local taxi driver now. He's ... tall ... handsome.

SUE: Oh, what's the point?

ALICE: The point is that anyone who owns land can do what they like with it, within reason.

SUE: But this preposterous thing he wants to build is not within reason. Do you know what this will do to the park? To the town? To the whole coast?

ALICE: Yes. It will turn the town into paradise. It will bring wealth and prosperity to the region. It will bring tourists who have money to spend. It will do all the good things that a development of this sort can bring.

SUE: Then if you won't help me save our park, I'll do it by myself.

ALICE: Good luck. But don't take this sort of thing too seriously. As I said, this town, all these towns along the coast, need development if they are to survive. Our town in particular has seen almost no growth in its population over the past few years. Other towns are the same. It can't go on.

SUE: I don't care. I'm not going to allow it to happen. [NEWSPAPER IS PICKED UP AND PAGES UNFOLDED] Just listen to it ... one hundred motel units ... houses ... cabins ... an eighteen-hole golf course ... a mini golf course, swimming pools, tennis courts, squash centre, a gymnasium.

ALICE: And where do you, or I should ask, where *would* you
            play squash, or tennis, or golf, or cricket, or go
            swimming?

SUE: That's not the point. The point is, this must not happen.
            Please, help me.

ALICE: I can't. I'll be away when all the action's taking place.
            Anyway, you ought to meet this guy, this Max Larsen ...
            I'm sure you'll like him. He is, as I said, rather dashing.
            And I think he likes you.

SUE: I don't care if he's got two heads and six legs and
            belongs in the local zoo.

ALICE: He doesn't belong in the local zoo, because we don't
            have one. The town's not progressive enough for a zoo,
            or for anything else. In fact, this is the first positive thing
            that's about to happen to the place since you and I were
            born. [pause] Do you realise this is the first time I can
            remember you losing your temper? That's progress!
            You ought to do it more often.

SUE: I will, but I won't do it just for you. I'll do it for the local
            taxi driver.

ALICE: Millionaire. He's a millionaire several times over. You
            should see his house on the hill above the park. And it's
            just as beaut inside as it is outside.

SUE: When have you been inside his house?

ALICE: Several times. He's invited me up for coffee, or a drink
            at odd times.

SUE: And you've accepted, of course.

ALICE: Get angry more often. It will do you good. Yes, as I said, he has invited me up for a drink. But that's all.

SUE: I don't care if that's all or not. The point is, you probably knew all about this development. You could at least have written to me about it. And just a few moments ago, you implied that you barely knew of this Larsen.

ALICE: I knew he had plans, but I didn't want to upset you unnecessarily just before your exams.

SUE: Well, you've upset me now.

ALICE: Listen, I'm only a few years older than you are, but I know there's nothing you can do. Now, lay off, and leave everything as it is.

SUE: I've only just begun. Anyway, you said that I should lose my temper more often.

ALICE: I didn't think you'd take me seriously. It might not go ahead anyway. It might be only an idea he has. He might forget about it tomorrow.

SUE: People don't forget ideas this big overnight. By tomorrow he might have expanded on the proposal.

ALICE: Listen, pop over and talk to Max. I know he'd rather like to meet you.

SUE: Don't bother. I'll handle him my way. I doubt whether anyone would be able to reason with him.

ALICE: I'm sure you could if you went up to see him. It might save you a lot of frustration.

SUE: That is something I refuse to do!

ALICE: Well, that doesn't matter, because I've arranged a party
           for you tomorrow evening at his house.

SUE: What! You're raving mad!

ALICE   I arranged it at his home, because he wanted to meet
           you. When I told him that I was throwing a party, and
           why, he asked me — almost pleaded with me — to let
           me have it at his place.

SUE: So you immediately agreed. Alice! What else do you
           know about him?

ALICE: Nothing much. He's been around town for many years,
           moved here to take over the taxi business, built that up
           from one cab to two, then to three, moved into real
           estate, then salvage operations, and now, it seems, he's
           launching himself into property development. That's all
           I know about him. Apart from that, well, he'd like to
           meet you.

SUE: Oh, sure!

ALICE: I'm off to get things now for the party. You will be there,
           won't you?

SUE: No. I mean yes. I will go and see him tomorrow
           evening. I will try to reason with him. I will try to make
           him change his mind. But I won't enjoy myself.

ALICE: You will. Quite frankly, I'm getting rather tired of
           hearing about this business. [pause] You'll have to
           excuse me for now because I have to make
           arrangements for your party and contact everyone who
           might like to see you again. That's the least I can do for
           you before I say farewell.

Reach For the Sky

SUE: Oh, I forgot about your going away.

ALICE: When I come back, I might be a different person. And so might you be, Susan. You might be different in many ways. You might show more tolerance, more understanding.

SUE: More understanding! I like that. If Max Larsen showed more understanding, then …

ALICE: I can't fight your battles for you. The flat will be yours, so don't forget to pay the rent each week. What you'll pay it with, I don't know. Perhaps the development will lead to a good job for you. But I guess I can do no more for now than to wish you luck. But for now, remember one thing. The majority of people in the town are in favour of this sort of thing. You seem to be the only person I've met recently who's opposed to development.

SUE: They're too busy watching their environment being destroyed. They won't take any action to stop it.

ALICE: I guess they feel there's not much they can do to stop it. Perhaps they're afraid.

SUE: Afraid of people like Larsen?

ALICE: He has a reputation of being tough. He won't let anything — or anyone — stand in his way. You're rather brave to even attempt to stand up to him. But please excuse me. I have to go and organize the party for tomorrow evening.

SFX: FADE UP SOUNDS OF A NOISY PARTY, HOLD THEN FADE TO OFF.

LARSEN: Ah, Susan. There is so much noise. And it is far too warm for us in here. Let's walk outside for a few moments.

SUE: Alright.

LARSEN: A drink?

SUE: Sherry.

SFX: GLASSES CLINKING. DOORS OPENING THEN CLOSING, PARTY NOISES; HOLD THEN FADE TO OFF.

SUE: Thanks.

LARSEN: I come out onto the balcony most nights to watch the lights of the town reflected in the water.

SUE: It is beautiful and quiet. At the moment.

SFX: MOTOR BOAT IN THE DISTANCE, HOLD THEN FADE TO OUT.

LARSEN: Indeed it is. And soon the moon will be coming up over the horizon. [pauses] I have often wondered how many people enjoy beauty, such as the moon rising above the water, and the sunsets in the evenings, or even the dawn itself. They are such simple pleasures.

SUE: Mmm.

LARSEN: Susan, I have heard that you have returned home for good this time? That at least is what I understand after talking with your sister recently.

SUE: Mr Larsen, I have no time for small talk. Now, what did you wish to discuss with me out here?

LARSEN: Hey, not so harshly. Please, relax, enjoy yourself. That is why I offered to make my home available to your sister for the party this evening. I suggested my home because I wanted to meet you and talk with you at length.

SUE: About what?

LARSEN: Oh, about many things we might have in common. I believe you appreciate this town very much but that is so obvious, because you have returned home after all these years.

SUE: Oh?

LARSEN: Alice has joked with me recently that you were perhaps not interested in meeting me. Well, I was hoping that your attitude towards me might have changed on this occasion.

SUE: Then I would suggest, Mr Larsen, that you think again. Thanks for the drink. I shall return inside.

LARSEN: Wait. There are things that need to be said.

SUE: If you insist. Since you're blocking the only doorway into the lounge room, I guess I have little choice. [pauses] Don't you think that a sensible debate would be worthwhile? Or, Mr Larsen, would you prefer no one to disapprove of your plans in public? Then you could boast that everyone approves of the development, and your scheme would get a free and unopposed run through the next Council meeting.

LARSEN: Susan, you clearly underestimate my intentions.

SUE: Why do you want to build such a monstrosity on that land? To ruin it? To remove the very tourist potential itself?

LARSEN: I don't think you need to fear anything.

SUE: Fear anything? You are about to ruin one of the few remaining pockets of such land in the district, and one of the last and most significant areas of its type in this region. And you tell me that I have nothing to fear?

LARSEN: Susan, I have no intentions of — as you imply — pulling down all the trees. I have no intentions of destroying that land any more than you would.

SUE: [exasperated] It's pointless trying to argue with you. I can see that quite clearly. But let me tell you this. I have no intentions of giving up my fight to save it from destruction.

LARSEN: I appreciate that parkland almost as much as you do.

SUE: An area that once was. That's all you'll be able to say about it. That it once was parkland. That it once was beautiful. That there once were birds there. And beautiful trees, and ... and people once walked there, and once enjoyed themselves.

LARSEN: Once ... once ... Susan, why not look to the future? I look ahead. There is no point in looking behind. We all know where we have been. Look ahead. That is the mystery. That's where the excitement lies. In the future. I like to make people happy.

SUE: You've been a miserable failure in that regard as far as I am concerned.

LARSEN: Well then, what would you like to see on that land?

SUE: I have known that land for nearly thirty years. I feel as if I grew up there. Last night, I went there and sat by the water's edge. It might well have been my very last opportunity to walk there unhindered! Perhaps, Mr Larsen, you have some objections to my trespassing on your very own piece of private land?

LARSEN: Not at all. But please go on.

SUE: Well, many other people go there as well. But of course, a developer such as yourself would not know what I'm talking about.

LARSEN: I know perfectly well what you are saying. I too have feelings, although sometimes I may appear to be a little insensitive to some people.

SUE: There's nothing more to say. Don't ruin it. Keep it for the people. It is theirs, you must realise.

LARSEN: It was public land, if that's what you mean. But it's now mine. The people gave up their claim to it. And that may be a good thing, as far as you and I are concerned. Obviously the Council was unable to look after it properly.

SUE: [vehemently] I haven't given up my claim to it! Not yet, and I won't either, for a very long time to come!

LARSEN: You appear over-sensitive to issues such as development.

SUE: I'm sensitive to the area because I love it so much. I don't think talking logically to you is going to make you change your mind. [pause] When do you propose to start building this monstrosity?

LARSEN: You are anxious to see it begin?

SUE: No, on the contrary, I want to know how much time I've got left to oppose it, and get it thrown out of Council, and hopefully, the land returned to its rightful owners.

LARSEN: [laughing] Then I may have to modify my plans a little.

SUE: Please do. Modify them so there are walkways through the parkland, and to the top of the hill, and down to the water, and across to the inlet, and from there to the cove on the other side of the hill. And incorporate a small jetty in the cove so people can arrive by boat.

SFX: DOOR OPENS, FADE PARTY SOUNDS UP AND HOLD.

LARSEN: Some of the guests are coming this way. Come, allow me to escort you through my home. There is much here that I wish you to see for yourself.

SFX: FADE OUT PARTY NOISES. FOOTSTEPS ON A WOODEN BALCONY, FADING TO OFF. DOOR OPENING AND CLOSING. FOOTSTEPS ALONG A CORRIDOR: HOLD THEN STOP.

SUE: Were these photographs hung here for my benefit? I mean, I didn't think you would have had any interest in sea birds, or tree frogs. Or in reptiles.

LARSEN: You are beginning to learn something about me already. See, we should not delay our acquaintance any longer. But in the meantime, come this way. There is so much to show you.

SFX: FOOTSTEPS ALONG CORRIDOR: HOLD THEN STOP.

SUE: For my benefit also? Did you place these conveniently around your house so you would make me think that you had some concern for our environment? Incidentally, who's the photographer?

LARSEN: These were taken by a special friend of mine. I will introduce you to her one day.

SUE: She does good work.

LARSEN: Yes, she does. She is very good. She has taught me a lot about photography. Particularly about nature photography. And about natural history itself.

SUE: I see.

SFX: FOOTSTEPS ALONG CORRIDOR. DOOR OPENING, THEN CLOSING. FOOTSTEPS; HOLD THEN STOP.

LARSEN: Come this way, I will show you something.

SFX: FOOTSTEPS ON A HARD SURFACE: HOLD THEN STOP.

LARSEN: This sun room allows both light and warmth through to the ferns and numerous orchids that I have growing in here. You are familiar with ferns?

SUE: Yes. I am.

LARSEN: This variety is from New Guinea.

SUE: You were there?

LARSEN: Only briefly. Business, that was all. But it didn't work out for me. In business. there are successes and failures.

SUE: Yes, like buying up the reserve and …

LARSEN: Say no more. That I regard as my greatest business deal
            yet accomplished.

SUE: What! You're impossible!

SFX: [OFF] CLOCK BELLS CHIME.

LARSEN: Perhaps I should reveal my plans to you, now that we
            are alone.

SUE: You already have. In the newspaper last week.

LARSEN: One must not believe everything one reads in the
            newspapers.

SUE: Then you're going to increase the size of the
            development? Maybe there will be two hundred units,
            an extra golf course or two, and a few other …

LARSEN: There will be nothing of the kind. I should now explain,
            especially since you are anxious about the land.

SUE: Go on.

LARSEN: The plans you have heard about … read about. They will
            not go ahead. Not now. Not next year. Never.

SUE: What!

LARSEN: As I said, one mustn't believe everything one reads —
            particularly in the local press. But I must ask you not to
            mention this to anyone.

SUE: That depends!

LARSEN: Let me take a chance, and gamble with you. You do not
            seem to be the type who would upset my real plans.

289

SUE: I wouldn't count on that, if I were you, Mr Larsen. But
            ... go on.

LARSEN: The Council, as you no doubt have guessed, is ... and
            has been for a long time ... short of money. They
            realised that they could get a lot of money by selling off
            land — reserves, and other unused land they have.

SUE: They have complained for many years that they have
            been short of money. I know that.

LARSEN: 'Short' is an understatement. They were on the verge of
            bankruptcy until only very recently. This reserve ... the
            land that you have enjoyed so much ... was for sale, so I
            spread rumours around the district that I wanted to buy
            it and develop it. I knew the Council would fall for that.
            They always do. How many times have you heard the
            phrase 'we must develop this area' or 'we must develop
            that area'?

SUE: Often. When I'm in town, that is.

LARSEN: A lot has been said about developments. [pause] I made
            it known that I would develop the land on a large scale.
            Everyone knows that I have the money to do so. So,
            there was no trouble buying the land from the Council.
            It was easy.

SUE: But ... the development?

LARSEN: If you read next week's paper, there would appear to be
            moves to develop it as you have described. And you
            will read the same sort of arguments for the next few
            months, at least.

SUE: But ... why ...

LARSEN: Why not develop the reserve? Answer this question, Susan. Would you want to look down on a hundred motel units, a conglomeration of cabins? And see the trees cleared to make way for another golf course in the town? I think not. And would you really like to live above an area — like I do — that is now quiet, and suddenly have the peace and tranquility transformed by rock bands every night? And have the sounds of the fishing vessels obliterated by the noise of traffic?

SUE: You have told the people you are going to develop this ... whatever one might call it.

LARSEN: Eventually I will tell the people I continue to hold discussions with the Council, and with the residents ... to make my bid look at least a little genuine. And a few months after that I will make some other statement — mainly for the benefit of the councilors — that I have negotiated with an architect to draw up some elaborate — and dreadfully ugly — plans. They'll love it!

SUE: And?

LARSEN: And then I'll forget about it. So will the Council, and so will the people. But I must apologise to you. As the titles were transferred to my name only late this afternoon, I couldn't reveal my real intentions any earlier.

SUE: I see.

LARSEN: Perhaps I could have told you a little earlier this evening, but unfortunately you would not give me the chance to do so.

SUE: Couldn't the Council resume the land once they find out that you won't develop it as you had told them?

LARSEN: That is why I referred to this as one of my greatest business successes. I have ensured that the Council will be unable to resume the land from me for any purpose. I have today asked my solicitor to have the land held in trust ... never to be developed ... never to be sold ... never to be resumed by them. But for now, we must go back to the party. The other guests will be wondering what I have done with you. It is, after all, your party. And I seem to have taken you away from your friends for the evening. You might like to see the rest of the house another time, and have lunch with me here? And walk through the parkland with me? Perhaps we could discuss a possible future for the land.

SUE: I ... I'd like that. Yes, I'd like that very much.

SFX: FADE UP PARTY NOISES, HOLD, THEN FADE TO OUT

CONCLUSION

This chapter should have given you some ideas about how to write your scripts for radio.

Remember, it is your program you are presenting. You can write the scripts for other interest groups that are under-represented in the media. These could be programs to inform, stimulate or bring together people with similar views — writers, environmentalists, conservationists or even those with political interests.

Public awareness can be broadened by publicity and explanation. Radio can bring together people of a particular persuasion and inform others of the latest issues affecting them.

There is, of course, a great range of programs that are possible. Create programs to inform people and share information with others. Remember that skills not used are skills that become lost. Talents not used are talents not shared.

GET INVOLVED IN COMMUNITY RADIO

It's easy to become involved in community radio. Locate your nearest radio station or pick the one you feel could offer you the best scope for your interests, and approach the station. Help out for a while, see how it's done, who does what, and find your own niche when air time becomes available.

All community radio stations run training courses for those interested in presenting programs. Take part in one of these to find out what the different knobs, sliders and dials on the console are for, how the equipment works, and why it works the way it does.

Community radio can be the starting point for launching you in a career in radio.

Chapter 15 Marketing Yourself

You're now a writer! Or, very shortly, you will be one, and I think you will be a good one. How do I know that?

That's easy. You have been keen enough to get this far in the book. You want to become a writer. And so you shall be a writer! A successful writer is one who never gives up, no matter how many rejections he or she gets from publishers and editors.

To be a good writer is one thing. To be a successful writer is another altogether.

A good writer is one who can write clearly, saying just the things he or she wants to say, using just the right words that are required to get the message across. If you are interested in writing fiction, then the same rules apply — you will use only the right words, conveying your message to readers so clearly, there will be no misunderstanding at all.

A successful writer is one who can make money from their writing, sell, hopefully, lots of books or be successful in any other way relating to writing, such as writing the text for effective websites, writing blogs, and lots of them, for other people.

Now it's your job to promote yourself, and your skills, to the rest of the world.

And you will really be promoting yourself to the rest of the world. Gone are the days when you would have worked in your own tiny little village, writing only for the local community. With the right promotion, you could reasonably expect contacts from anywhere in the world. This is no exaggeration. Even with samples of articles I have had published, I get readers call up my site from all over the world—anywhere in Europe, the United States, Asia.

The most effective method of reaching the rest of the world is through the use of the World Wide Web—better known as the Internet.

From now on, forget the concept of 'small'. Your market is as large as you want to make it. If you have written in the right genre, clearly, effectively, and you can turn around other clients' work in a short time, there is no reason why you should not be targeting the world.

It sounds grandiose, I know, but this concept is not far-fetched. It is the real world, and you are now part of it. It is only unsuccessful people now who will try to hold you back, put you down and try to keep you just like they are —at the bottom, with few prospects of ever rising above that level.

A friend likes to send me inspirational emails because she knows I appreciate them. She sent me one recently that sums up this attitude perfectly. It was from George Bernard

Shaw, who said that you will always get criticism from those who are unable to do the things that you are doing.

How true.

You will write the text for a website, send the website to the top of the search engine results, and you can expect comments like 'I would never have said that ...' No, they are right, they wouldn't have said that, because they are probably incapable of writing anything meaningful.

'I would never read a book like that, so you are unlikely to sell many books.' 'I don't know why you bothered.' Yes, they do say things like that — I get comments of this nature all the time. Most writers do — until people realise that the writers take no notice of them and they are wasting their time giving good writers such fantastic insight into their own lack of creativity.

So if you get similar comments, just quote George Bernard Shaw to them. You should notice an immediate change in their attitude. They will go away and you will be able to get on with worthwhile matters, such as promoting yourself, or your book or books. Remember that people like these only serve to slow you down and drag you down to their level. Get rid of them, because they serve little purpose.

What do you put in your website that is going to be available right around the whole world? It depends on the type of writing you wish to specialise in. It might be the text for effective websites — websites that get the message across to readers, and command results. How many businesses can you think of who would appreciate a website for themselves that can do this? Probably all of them.

You might be a writer, and will be promoting your new book on carpentry projects for the home, or making pavlovas.

Start with a good, simple, clear design. Readers don't want a complex site when they call up a page. They just want the facts. Eliminate the thought of including any bells and whistles—they slow down the website when it is loading, and usually provide very little useful input. If your site looks promising to them in the first ten to fifteen seconds, then they will probably read on.

Yes, that's all the time you will have these days to get your message across, tell readers that you are the person they should be contacting to help them. Be bold. Be audacious.

Then you can tell them why they should make contact with you.

For a new writer, you should have at least one page each to introduce yourself, your project, your book, and what it will mean to them if they make contact with you, and you should encourage them to buy your book.

So if you are promoting yourself as a great web writer, then your website should appear on the first page—second page at the most—of the major search engines. This will ensure that readers can find you easily.

Another page will be needed to promote your services as a writer—if you are specialising in one or two aspects of writing, such as web writing or writing blogs, then one page should be dedicated to this.

And if a person is dealing with someone they have never met, perhaps have never heard of until now, then they will want to know about you. Yes, you, as a person;

you, as an individual. Keep it simple, keep it brief but make sure you include all relevant aspects of how good you are. It won't be necessary to include your whole resume, particularly if many parts of that don't really pertain to the book or to your expertise in writing the book you are promoting. You want them to engage with you. You, whom they have never met. Tell readers what you are about. If you have written a how-to book about your favourite hobby, then tell them how many projects you have made, that you have a home workshop, that you work with the local community to put together projects for your community, then they can relate to all this. Make yourself sound human!

If your book is about making pavlovas, and you have won prizes for your cooking in regional shows, your readers will want to know about your expertise. Include photographs of the pavlovas you have made, and photographs of the prizes you have won.

If you are promoting a book, then the potential reader will want to know about the book. How many pages does it have? How much does it cost. Where can they buy a copy? When was it published? How many chapters does it have?

Even if you have the most fantastic website and don't want to touch a thing on it for the next five years, you can still update the content by having a blog page. See Chapter 12 on writing for the web.

Become an expert in your field of writing. Become known as 'the author of that book about carpentry projects I have read about'. This makes you an authority, and people are more inclined to buy your book if they believe that you know what you are saying.

Have on your website somewhere where they can connect with you, and can perhaps connect with other readers who might be interested in discussing the topic of your book. It might only be a 'shout box' or a forum section. If people feel you are open and can respond to them, they are more likely to engage with you. Once you have them engaging with you, they are more likely to buy your book. Many people engage with Facebook pages and Twitter and other social media sites as part of their marketing campaign.

You will probably have put a lot of effort into writing your book. Don't let the subject rest there.

If readers can subscribe to a regular newsletter that you produce, this is to your benefit. If they can get the first issue free, they can have a read of its content. If they feel the newsletter is going to have value for them and is going to be interesting, they are more likely to subscribe to future issues. People love to receive something for nothing. A free newsletter—even the first issue—is something they will value and appreciate.

The regular newsletter is going to push you along as an expert, as the writer of your book, and obviously as someone who knows their subject well.

With newsletters and the right software, you shouldn't have to spend weeks preparing the material. You could have reviews of new tools, reviews of new books about the subject of your book. You could have instructions from other readers. They will appreciate being given the opportunity to include their little articles in a newsletter and see them out there for the rest of the world to read. Put in a highlighted paragraph to the effect that contributions from readers would be appreciated. Give them some guidelines — how long you want the articles, how many photographs, how many line drawings and so on.

Good newsletters don't happen overnight. There is a surprising amount of work and time and effort needed to produce a newsletter of sufficient standard that readers will want to go to it for information, and hopefully buy your book.

Chapter 9 covers the topic of writing magazine articles. Use this information to structure your newsletter articles.

To begin with, possibly eight pages would be a good start. Be prepared to expand it if you get sufficient material, and enough material on a regular basis to ensure that you can produce the newsletter with the frequency you have stated on each copy, and on your website.

Don't get caught out the day before you are due to put the next issue of your newsletter on line and find you have enough copy for half a page — you now need another seven and a half pages. Where do you find that in a hurry?

When you write the first issue, and are happy with its content, begin preparing the next issue straight away. If you are three months ahead of production, this will be good. You won't need to write all the content in one sitting. If yours is a quarterly newsletter, you will have almost three months to write eight pages — not a great deal of effort is required for that. That's one page in one and a half weeks. Again, that is easy to do.

The good thing with asking readers to contribute is that you should have a surplus of material. You will be able to sort out the quality information from the material that is not of the same standard. With the latter, you can either edit it heavily, or rewrite it. If you re-write the contribution, still give the contributor credit for their work. Don't rewrite their material and put your name on it. That is definitely a no-no!

If you can get the community to write material for the newsletters, that will save you a lot of time. It frees up time you can then spend writing your next book, or gives you more time to make sure the newsletter is produced to a high standard.

Don't expect to sell thousands of books in the first week, despite having the best website, the best blogs, and the best newsletter to be found anywhere on the Internet.

It just does not happen that way.

It takes time for all the information to filter down through other websites, with their links.

With time, if the material you are offering is really worth reading, you will find your newsletter appearing as a link to so many other sites. Readers will find your site. They may not even comment to you directly (they usually don't), but they will link the newsletter or your book to their website so their own readers can gain valuable information. That is why it is so important to ensure that your website, your blogs and particularly your newsletters contain only good quality information, written well and free of mistakes.

To convey the impression that you are a real person, and you really are sitting there ready to respond to readers questions, always make sure you respond to their emails. If you don't you could expect to see an entry on some remote site to the effect that you don't even respond to questions. In other words, you are not even interested in them. Make sure you are interested in them — they are your clients. They are the potential buyers of your book. And if you bring out another book or two, and you have a good relation with them, they are more likely to visit your page, see your new book promoted in your regular newsletter, and buy a copy.

Join community forums that engage in discussions that relate to the subject of your book. This will provide good publicity, and most of the time, they will be free.

The members of these forums are wanting information, how-to hints, or they want to solve a problem they have.

This is an important area where you can make a valuable contribution to their discussion, and at the same time build yourself up. You would be seen as someone who is willing to spend time helping others. This is important with readers. You will be seen as someone with expertise in your chosen subject. You might already be an expert, but you can still give to others, and give to your on-line community. And if you contribute often enough, your name will become familiar to all those joining in the discussions in the forums. If they know you exist, guess what that could lead to?

An important tool for promoting your books and your expertise is through a short video uploaded to YouTube. This doesn't cost you anything, but the returns could be enormous. Get someone to record a three- to five-minute video of you demonstrating some aspect that is covered in your book. YouTube attracts hundreds of millions of viewers every month. Your video could be viewed by millions of people. How many sales of your book could that lead to?

There are so many things you can do to promote yourself, and to promote your book. You will most likely find that writing the book in the first place was the easiest part of all and the least time consuming.

Without any promotion, without proper and effective marketing, you book is going nowhere!

Chapter 16 Self-Publishing

Wow! Remember the time a couple of decades ago when you could walk into a book store and buy a book about just about anything?

Have you tried that lately? Have you even tried to find a book store? If you have, you will probably have realised that there are far fewer book stores around than there were decades ago. That's not because people don't still enjoy reading—just the opposite. It seems to be a matter of ...

Well, there are numerous factors responsible for the demise of book stores around the world. Many huge chains of book stores have closed, including Borders, and Barnes and Noble. Many smaller publishers who regarded new writers favourably have been gobbled up by the bigger publishing houses, which in turn have disappeared within even bigger publishing houses. Just the other day (at the time of writing), Penguin and Random House had joined forces. This does not create more opportunities for writers, but probably less and with less chances of getting a manuscript accepted.

In the past, many writers who have dealt with

mainstream publishers (myself included) have been very disappointed with the performance of some of them.

With takeovers, your own book that had been doing rather well will suddenly be remaindered, or sold off at cost with no further royalties due to you because a larger publisher wanted to eliminate the competition. The result? Exit your book from the shelves of book stores, to be found weeks later selling for three dollars at stores that handle remaindered copies sold to them cheaply by the publishers.

Even when publishers did the right thing by authors, and when book stores did the right thing in turn by the publishers, there were often problems. Book stores were allowed to order a certain number of books. If they hadn't sold them within a reasonable time, were permitted to return them to the publisher. Hence, no royalties for the author on those copies that were returned.

One can understand the attitude of book stores. New books are arriving almost every day. To make room for new titles, older ones (even those only six months old) had to be removed from the shelves to make room for the new titles.

Often books would not be found in the appropriate place in bookshops. Managers would often go on the title alone without realising the book had little to do with the title. A book with the title *Fly With Me Now* might be about motivation, not aviation. Or it could be about setting up your own business. How could any purchaser hope to find your book that is so out of place?

In those good old days of having a book published by a mainstream publisher, the time lag from finishing your manuscript, sending proposal after proposal to any number of publishers, could be measured in years—allowing three months for each proposal to be considered and rejected, and sent to the next publisher, to wait three months, to have it rejected, to send it ...

If, after sometimes a couple of years, you did hit the big time and score yourself a contract, that was not the end of the waiting, perhaps only a further delay in the publishing process. I once waited two and a half years from signing the contract with a smaller publisher to seeing the first copies of the book delivered to my letterbox.

An author would receive an advance on royalties. These were usually determined by the normal royalty (usually around ten percent of the retail price), multiplied by the number of copies the publisher was confident of selling within a reasonable time.

Not a great return on the investment of your time in writing the manuscript! And then there were marketing problems. The author had to travel the country, sometimes the world, to promote his book. If it had the potential to become a big seller, it would have been worth the efforts of the author to do this.

However, and this is a big however ... the return on many, if not most, books, is small by any standard. You might, in countries such as Australia, sell two thousand books, with a royalty of two or three dollars a copy, giving you a month's meagre income for what could have been twelve months intensive work.

That's the negative side of publishing. Some authors who became well known made it by giving up on mainstream publishers and self-publishing their books. On occasions, a large publisher would get a copy of the book, see how it was turning out, and agree to publish the title under their own imprint. It has happened that way, but not very often.

Other authors moved away from mainstream publishers and self-published their works, to be rewarded handsomely. Others self-published their work, only to find they had a lounge room or the spare bedroom in the house full of cartons of their unsold books.

There are many horror stories about publishing. If you are interested in reading about more stories, try to locate the book *The Awful Truth About Publishing*, by John Boswell. His book is enough to scare any would-be author out of trying to get one book published.

PRINT-ON-DEMAND

There is a much-used saying to the effect that when a door closes, another door opens.

The doors in the publishing industry have been not only closing, but many have been slamming shut, their hinges rusted to the door frames, never to be opened again.

That's the bad news. For every bad story about the 'old' way of publishing, there are many stories about the new way of getting published.

With the latest technology, the easy-to-use software, and with a computer being almost standard in most households, and a part of just about every business, you, as author, can take care of your own writing, publishing, and distribution and marketing. Hasn't the world moved on in just a few years?

You know the book you have just written better than anyone else. After all, you wrote it, so you should understand all about it. You know the market, because you wrote the book for your own readers. Remember what I said in Chapter One about writing it for a particular reader?

The new trend of publishing books includes you the writer, you the publisher, and you the marketing manager, and you the promotions manager, and you involved with just about every other aspect of your book.

The idea of self-publishing, using digital printing coupled with print-on-demand printing (often abbreviated to POD) is the way modern writers are turning. Within this category, there are some companies that will do all the work for you, including designing the text pages, designing the cover, printing, marketing, distribution. You will pay them a large sum up front, get a couple of free copies of your book, and wait for the company to sell your book.

There are now numerous firms specialising in print-on-demand publishing. Check the Internet. Others are appearing on-line all the time. Some of these companies will design the book for you (for a fee), design a cover for your book (again, for a fee), and get it ready for printing and them print off as many copies as are required or as many as you order at any one time.

While I have found one such company to offer good service, with quality printing, prompt turnaround time, other writers using the same company to publish their work have not been able to make similar recommendations. Consider them all. More importantly, look for reviews of the service provided by all of them. I came across the reviews (many of them, in fact) for one such firm. The main complaints were that the service was slow, the books fell to pieces on the first reading, postage was expensive, and a few other complaints users had experienced.

No company will provide perfect service in everyone's mind, there will always be someone who feels put out by some little thing that went wrong, but you can gauge the general mood of those using each POD company to see how they are performing. It is important to realise that some might start off badly, be taken over and the new management will send that company to the top of the preferred list. Those reviews you read about might refer to sub-standard service and products that no longer apply. Try to look for recent reviews.

This is the age of the Internet, and it is the age of fast-moving technology. The things that are said about a business today might be out of date next week. With the use of the Internet, where anyone can make a comment, most businesses are striving to be better than everyone else, so they are evolving to perfection. Their genes might suffer a hiccup from time to time, but that applies to our bad days too, doesn't it?

With other POD companies, you can do all the design work yourself if you prefer to. Or you can upload the text as a Word document and it is converted into a PDF ready for printing. Unfortunately with that procedure, you do not have any control over how it will look when it is published. Whichever option you choose, look carefully at the first copy you buy, check it for all its faults (on the first printout it will have many) and upload the corrected work as required.

Some companies claim they send out emails to tens of thousands of potential clients who will all be eager to buy your book. Unfortunately, the take-up rate from emails blasting in-boxes every day is minuscule, as you have probably realised as you delete most emails asking you to buy something.

For a couple of thousand dollars, there is no guarantee they will sell enough books to cover the cost of production, even with their so-called marketing efforts.

The next option is the one that I like, and is the one I encourage other writers to consider.

Consider this in a logical step-by-step process.

Buy the right software. Having tried the most expensive software on the market that was supposed to have been the perfect solution, I have ditched the software because it was so complicated to use. I don't need to mention its name — just look for the most expensive desktop publishing software and you are sure to find it.

Instead, I use Serif PagePlus8, which you can buy on-line (www.serif.com). I can assure you that I am not getting any commission or any other spin-offs from Serif but I am recommending their product because, over several years, I have found that it will do everything I want of it, it works all the time without freezing up the computer, is realistically affordable, and does an excellent job. You can save the work in PDF format that is suitable for printing as well as viewing on computer screens and tablets and mobile devices a well as other e-book readers, and as e-pub and other formats for some of the more popular readers. Also by using PagePlus to publish your books as e-books, you can save your work for distribution in any of the usual formats, not only as PDF books. So imagine what I would be saying to praise it up if Serif were paying me!

With whichever software you choose, set up the page

size you want, whether A4, A5 or some other size that you think would work well for your book.

You set the master page for all the fine trimmings — font style and size, font for headings, styles, styles for quotes, inserts, and everything else you want to include in your book.

You bring the text into text frames.

I recommend that you spend perhaps several hours learning to use the software so that you can make it sing. Good software will do everything you want it to do for you, as long as you know what it will do, and what you have to set for this to happen. With the right software, you are really limited by your own imagination. Even for an author whose imagination does not extend far beyond his text, there are numerous templates for you to use, and many instructions in the help sections that accompany the software so you would find it very difficult not to get it right.

If your book has several long chapters, it might be easier to work with if you treat each chapter separately, rather than making the book one huge volume. The reason I suggest that is that if you put headers and titles of chapters and book titles on alternative pages, these can be thrown out of sequence if you need to add or delete blocks of text.

If your book has illustrations, drawings or photographs, the text flows around the pictures after you have designated how much space to allow each picture and how you want the text to flow. If your book has a lot of illustrations, publish the book in PDF format as all pictures, diagrams and photographs stay in the right place. With e-book formats, the text varies according to the width of the reader's screen, so the illustrations might not come out where you entered them.

Set in the footer the page number, and the software will add sequential page numbers even when separate chapters are brought together at the end.

You now have the basis of your book, but you are far from finished with it yet.

Your book will require the title pages and preliminaries, often referred to as the prelims. This section will usually be unnumbered, or they might have a different style of numbering, such as Latin numerals, if you choose to number them at all. Whether they are numbered or not, they must still be taken into account in the total page numbering. Even if your prelims are not numbered, your main text might get started on perhaps page seven, or page nine.

In this section, you will need the title page. Here, include the title in big, bold letters so it stands out.

Under the title, add the sub-title of the book if you have one, put your name or pseudonym if you write under a pen name, and the name of the publisher you are going under.

On the next page, the title verso page, you will have the copyright notice with your name as the copyright owner, the year you first published it, the ISBN, and Cataloguing -in-Production data that you will obtain from the main national library in your country.

The next page will include author information—who you are, what your expertise is in writing the book. Keep it short—maybe one or two paragraphs will be sufficient.

If this is your first book, skip the 'Other books by the

author' page. If this is not your first book, then include them all.

ISBNs

To obtain your ISBN — and they really are essential if you are serious about publishing your work — check on the national library site in your country and see where you need to apply for an ISBN. In Australia, the United States of America, and some other countries, it is through Thorpe-Bowker, and they may deal with such numbers in others countries as well.

Why is the ISBN essential? Once you have that, and you submit copies as required for legal holdings to your national library, or libraries, your book will get into the database and in the books-in-print catalogues, and its existence will be circulated far and wide. Libraries and bookshops around the world will be able to find your publication. You can publish a book without an ISBN, and without submitting it to the legal deposits, but you would effectively be wasting your time.

What format will you be publishing your book in? If you will be producing it as a print book, you will need one ISBN. If you are also producing it as an e-book in PDF format, you will need another ISBN. If you will be bringing your book out as an e-pub, then a third ISBN registration will be required, with the same procedure needed for each number.

Some print-on-demand publishers will allocate you an ISBN, but don't be fooled by this. If libraries regard your book as merely a short-run print-on-demand book, you could find that the title is not included in databases, and so you will miss out on possibly the most efficient way of getting your book known to the users who count — such as libraries and book stores.

YOUR BUSINESS NAME

To get your own ISBN, think of the business name you will use for the publishing side of your book, or books.

Register that as a business. That will give you rights to use that name perhaps in a particular state, or perhaps a country. In countries like New Zealand, registration of a business name is not required, but you can lose the name easily by someone registering a trade mark for that same name or setting up a company with the name you wanted to use.

The trade mark is the safest option. It gives you exclusive use of that name for ten years at a time, renewable before expiry of each ten year period. You can take out a trademark in your country of residence, or any number of countries. If you register the trade mark in more than your home country, the registration in other countries should be done at the same time.

The whole registration process takes roughly seven months, because there is a long process through which the name is registered, so plan the publication process of your book well in advance. Other businesses that might be using the name, and have perhaps been using the name for years, would be entitled to appeal against your application. If there is no opposition, the name has to be publicised to allow for any appeals. If there is no opposition, and if there are no appeals to your application, the name is yours to use.

That name becomes the name of the publisher when applying for ISBNs.

Once you have the ISBN for a particular book, apply through your national library for cataloguing-in-production data. You should do this when you have almost completed the entire book, because you will have to include in the data submitted a copy of the front cover, the number of pages, and perhaps a copy of the text as a PDF so that your book can be indexed. This sets the registration process going, and makes the library aware of its pending release.

BOOK FORMATS

There are more and more formats in which you could publish your e-book other than PDF. PDF is good because it keeps the formatting exactly as you planned it. Other formats are good where there is nearly all text, such as a book of short stories or a novel. These formats include e-pub that is good for mobile telephones (smart phones) and tablets, although PDF formats are good for tablets too. With formats other than PDF, the reader does not have to enlarge every line of text or scroll through each line – the text flows. And with so many people owning a smart phone these days, and that number is increasing exponentially every year, make sure your book is available in one of the formats that will handle the book for such devices.

These days, converting a file to PDF is easy, as such capability comes built in to the software. There are also several standards of quality too for converting files to PDF. If your manuscript is small – smaller than a few megabytes, you should use the highest quality possible. If your book finishes at around three hundred megabytes, you might have to go to a lesser quality so uploading is not beyond the limits of the service available.

When converting the file to PDF, you might have the option of including cropping marks. Do not use them. The printer will not use them, and they might appear on your pages. Keep the text clean, and nothing too close to the margins, not even the page number. Allow plenty of space in the margins just in case they are printed and trimmed too close to one margin rather than being centred on the page.

With the print-on-demand service, you also need to consider price. Some offer good service, and the cost per book decreases with a larger number of books you buy. With some of the POD printers, all you need to buy is only one copy, maybe five copies.

If your book takes off and sells as well as I hope it does for you, then you can order more and more copies each time. Make sure you keep an adequate supply of them on hand.

COVERS

Covers can be a problem for a first-time author, but if you use the right software, you should be able to feel your way through the process of creating an effective cover that reflects the nature of the book you have written.

If your book is more than about eighty to one hundred pages long, you will need the title of the book, your name and the name of the publisher on the spine.

You will also need a blurb. This is the information about the book that is printed on the back cover. Here, you can be creative, because it is often the first part of the book readers will turn to when they want to assess any book. If that sounds inviting, they will look at the contents to see if the book contains what they are looking for. If that passes their assessment, they will read some of the contents.

On the back cover, you will also need a bar code with the ISBN. You can get one created for your book, or you can download software that will create the bar code for you. That usually goes on the bottom right corner of the back cover.

You will need author information on the back cover — who you are, and your expertise in writing the book.

When you have received your first copies, and are happy with them, submit the required number of copies to the national library in your country, and to your state library if required. Each country will have different requirements regarding the submission process, and in the number of copies they require.

By using print on demand services, you are still in control of your book, or books, you manage everything, and your lounge room is not cluttered with cartons of unsold books that are going to remind you, and worse still, remind your friends and family, about how you overestimated your literary talents. How embarrassing if you still have one thousand nine hundred and ninety books left out of the order for two thousand, if they were not successful!

Such companies also make books available as e-books in various formats for immediate download. People order the book, make the payment, and the book is downloaded into their computer, mobile phone or tablet. It's so easy!

BOOK PROMOTION

Promotion is next. There are outlets such as Amazon and others that will do distribution for you. Even many of the print-on-demand companies will help distribute your book for you, either through their own website, getting your titles listed in various directories, and by getting the book included in Amazon's database. If a reader goes to your website, likes the sound of your book and wants a copy, give them a link on your website where they can obtain a copy.

If you are selling books directly from your own website, you could make purchasing them easier for the buyer by having a 'buy now' button, and make payment go through a company such as PayPal that takes payment and passes this on to you.

And for e-books, this would be the best way to distribute them, although other companies, even the print-on-demand publishers, will be able to sell your e-books for you and pass on the payments they receive.

Chapter 17 Over To You

That's about all there is to being a writer — becoming the writer you have always wanted to be. Good writing develops from that first wish you might have had to become a writer. You will have chosen this option above all else, in preference to anything else you could have chosen. You really wanted to become a writer, and so you shall.

I once attended a writers workshop where the guest speaker for the evening was someone who was in the Guinness Book of Records. But while we did not envy his fame, we did all admire his tenacity. He was included in the Book of Records as being the least successful writer. At the time, his manuscript had been rejected sixty-two times. He had earned fifty cents from his writing—he had sold a couple of pages of photocopying for someone. Others, though, since that time, have far exceeded his record, but nevertheless they have gone on to make it into the world of published authors. Not one of these authors ever gave up. They realised the real world didn't believe in them, or in their talents, but they believed in themselves, and this is what made all the difference to them and to their success.

At the workshop, he gave each of us a copy of his book that he had had rejected so many times (he ended up self-publishing the book himself).

I never throw out books—I love them too much. But that book gave me a warm feeling. I used it to light the fire after I had read the first few pages. It was unreadable.

Quite a few years later, I was staying in the city where I first learnt about that particular author. I overheard someone talking enthusiastically about writing, the merits of writing, what it takes to become a writer. The person I was listening to behind me was the same man, who was talking to several others about his chosen way of life.

This author, despite his continued failure and despite his record number of rejections for the one manuscript, had that one quality that will make anyone a writer. He never gave up on what he wanted to become.

The same will apply to anyone else who wants to become a writer. If they never, never, never give up, there is a good chance they will become writers.

Writing is about that magical ingredient in life—personal achievement. It's what you want to get out of the process of putting words together to make a meaningful piece of writing, whether that writing is a blog for a website, a short story, a novel or any other genre of writing. Tenacity is that one magic ingredient that will make all successful writers stand out from those who never get their works into print.

Good writers have much passion for what they want to achieve in life. Pursuing their passion of writing makes good sense. For some writers, passion means being naturally talented or skilled at something they want to do. Without passion, writing is just another job, and I am sure many of us are aware of how we feel about just another job, especially one that pays as badly as writing does.

Passion is that ingredient in the whole writing process that makes us lose our sense of time and place and self. It's that magic ingredient that makes us forget about everything else that we would normally feel guilty about not doing. When you begin writing, you necessarily become good at it. Skill is something you acquire over time, and with tonnes and tonnes of practice.

Writing is not easy. It never was. It never will be. Good writing comes with difficulty to nearly all writers. Be patient in your undertakings. Be prepared to re-work your writing as often as you need to. Be prepared to spend a lot of time getting your story or your text just the way you want it, easy to read, meaningful, so it brings amusement, enjoyment or the impact to your readers you had intended. Not all are so gifted they can write one draft, send it to the publisher and get by return mail a publishing contract. It seldom works that way, although there might be one or two who are so gifted. If only! I am sure we would all turn into very good writers.

That doesn't mean that you can't continually improve your craft. Write as often as you can. Write from the heart. Write it as you feel inspired. When the urge to put those words onto your computer or your tablet overwhelms you, that's the time to make a meaningful impact on your journey to becoming the writer you have always wanted to be. But just put the words down ... anywhere for now. If it's not convenient to include them in your computer at the time, at least put them down somewhere ... anywhere ... perhaps in that writers notebook you have got into the habit of carrying everywhere with you. Tidy them up later. What they look like, what they sound like doesn't matter at first. It's what you do with those words later on that is so important.

If you strive for improvement, you will achieve just that. Even if you aim for small, incremental improvements to your writing each time you write, just imagine how much those small enhancements amount to over a year or two. The more you write, the better you will be. The more you improve on your previous attempts, the better you will become. The better you become, the more successful you will be as a writer.

Maybe you will ask yourself a silly question—the question of whether what you are writing really matters. If you are not sure, you will always have doubts. Is that short story, the article, the play, the novel, the romance, really worth the trouble, or are you going to ask if it is even worthwhile? Does the world really need another short story? Why should you be the one to bother with it, considering the amount of time it is going to take you to write it?

Can you imagine the world if every writer, every artist, every actor, asked themselves the same question—is it worth my time doing this? We would not have had the great literature handed down to us from those great writers of the past—Victor Hugo, Voltaire, Shakespeare, Yeats and the other great poets whose work is still read and admired and appreciated today.

There is only meaning to everything we do if we we

make it meaningful. If it is meaningful to us, then surely it must become meaningful to at least some other people of this world? We make our own meaning by seizing meaningful opportunities. For many of us, creativity is one of those meaningful opportunities.

Why shouldn't we make ourselves proud when we turn to the creative projects we say that we want to tackle? Making ourselves proud is what we are actually after in life, to achieve what we set out to achieve.

Writing, according to some authors, is a spiritual process—one where nothing else interests us more. Creativity, as hard as it is sometimes, also provide us with joy and happiness.

Given how hard so many people are finding it to stick with their creativity, it is amazing that the world has so many writers, and so many excellent authors.

If creativity is one of our life purposes, something we believe in because we believe in ourselves, then it is physically and mentally good for us to create something unique. All original writing is unique.

Does the end result of your writing make you happy? Then writing must be worthwhile—at least to you.

All good writers have one thing in common. They believe in themselves. It's what they want to do, usually above all else. And they won't accept anything less than their goal. Think of that record-breaking author. He never gave up. It's not your role in life to give up either.

That's really what makes a good writer. A good writer will never give up. He or she will never take no from a publisher or an editor. A good writer will disregard all the trivial criticism from those who can't write and will move ahead anyway in the direction of their dreams. So go for it. Become the writer you have always wanted to be.

Further Reading

Andrews, G J, 2014, *Easy Guide To Creative Writing*, Flairnet

Andrews, G J, 2014, *Easy Guide To Science and Technical Writing*, Flairnet

Andrews, G J, 2014, *You're On Air*, Flairnet

Boswell, J, 1986, *The Awful Truth About Publishing*, Warner Books

Collins, 2007, *Need To Know? Writing Fiction*, Collins

Evans, C H, 1991, *Writing For Radio*, W H Allen and Co

Grenville, K, 1990, *The Writing Book*, Allen and Unwin

Kane, T S, 1983, *The Oxford Guide To Writing*, Oxford University Press

Maisel, E, 2005, *A Writer's Paris*, Writers Digest Books

Mansfield, K, 2007, *The Collected Stories of Katherine Mansfield*, Penguin Books

Morris J & Lancaster M, 1985, *Writing Freelance Articles For Newspapers and Magazines*, Interface Publications Limited

Plotnik, A, 1982, *The Elements of Editing*, Macmillan Publishing Company

Richards, K, 1991, *Writing Radio Drama*, Currency Press

Santoro, A & Male, M, 2009, *Get Your Book Off the Ground*, The Writers' Resource Centre

Smiley, J, 2006, *13 Ways of Looking At the Novel*, Faber and Faber

Tredinnick, M, 2008, *Writing Well. The Essential Guide*, Cambridge

Index